Redwc

MW01097330

A Guide to Redwood
National and State Parks
California

Produced by the
Division of Publications
National Park Service

U.S. Department of the Interior
Washington, D.C.

Using This Handbook
Redwood National and State Parks protect ancient redwood forests and wild Pacific coastline. Part 1 of this
handbook introduces the parks and the movement to protect the world's tallest trees. Part 2 explores redwood natural history, the work restoring logged lands, and North
Coast Indian culture. Part 3 provides a travel guide and
reference materials for touring the parks.

National Park Handbooks are published to support
National Park Service management programs and promote understanding and enjoyment of the over 390
National Park System sites, which preserve important parts of our nation's natural and cultural
inheritance. They are sold at parks and can be
purchased by mail from: Superintendent of
Documents, U.S. Government Printing Office,
Stop SSOP, Washington, DC 20402-0001 or at
bookstore.gpo.gov. This is handbook number 154.

Part 1

Welcome to Redwood

Progress and Stability In the Woods

David Rains Wallace

Like fluted pillars, coast redwoods seem to emerge from a blanket of lifting fog in the forest understory (left).

Preceding pages and cover: *Schoolhouse Peak peers over fog to afford views of the distant redwoods and the Coast Ranges (contents pages). Bracken and sword ferns edge a quiet trail through Lady Bird Johnson Grove (pages 4-5). A green tree frog holds fast to delicate rhododendron petals (pages 6-7). With sheer delicacy, forest floor plants in Jedediah Smith Redwoods State Park's Stout Grove rivet attention despite the trees' contrasting bold bulk (pages 8-9 and front cover).*

The tallest living things can be surprisingly inconspicuous in their natural surroundings. I once stood on a ridgetop overlooking Redwood Creek, where the tallest redwood trees in the world grow, and saw not a single redwood. Fog hid them, as it does on many mornings and evenings. I had to walk for an hour down the steep, grassy "prairie" that crowned the ridge before something big and dark began to emerge from the gray blanket of mist. Even then, the fog would not allow me a clear look at the trees until I was underneath them, and it was too late to see them whole. I saw only gray, fluted pillars looming out of the tanoaks and rhododendrons of the forest understory. The pillars hardly seemed like trees in the conventional sense. They seemed somehow more than bark-covered wood, although exactly what more, I could not say. Others have felt this about redwoods. Gold Rush storyteller Bret Harte, who lived on California's North Coast in the 1850s, wrote of "a weird twilight that did not come from the outer world, but seemed born of the wood itself." Unclarities seem typical of *Sequoia sempervirens* and its foggy world.

Today, more than 95 percent of the original old-growth redwoods stand no more. People have wanted to protect them for different, sometimes conflicting, reasons—and disagreed about how to do it. In fact, the coast redwoods' complicated story says a lot about conflicts between progress, stability, and other values that have beset American civilization in the past century. Redwood National Park has been at the heart of the story, even though it was not established as a national park *per se* until near the end.

White explorers were not the first people to feel uncertainties about the giant trees that covered most of the North Coast two centuries ago. The native peoples were and are in awe of redwoods, spending most of their time on the seashores, rivers, and prairies on the edge of the forest. They used fallen

11

logs to make houses, boats, and furniture but seldom cut live ones. Early European explorers seemed, from their writings at least, oddly oblivious to the trees' grandeur. Even Archibald Menzies, the botanist who in 1794 collected the type specimen from which the species was named, left no memorable writing about the trees. In 1831 the pioneering botanist David Douglas did call the redwood "the great beauty of California. . . which gives to the mountain a peculiar—I was going to say *awful*—appearance, something that tells us we are not in Europe."

Although the Russian colony at Fort Ross was milling redwoods for lumber in the 1820s, early American settlers to California's North Coast regarded the soft, relatively brittle wood as inferior and imported building lumber from the East. They burned the forest on coastal flats to make fields and pastures. Carpenters soon discovered the redwood's immense durability and workability, however, and logging was underway from the Santa Cruz mountains to Mendocino County by the 1850s. Amid this din of axes and saws, a few voices were raised for redwood protection. California legislator Henry A. Crabb called for a redwood national park in 1852, and U.S. Secretary of the Interior Carl Schurz advocated withdrawal of some redwood land from sale or disposition in 1879. Yet the idea of not exploiting such a valuable resource simply seems not to have occurred to many people. Was the redwood's beauty not sufficient to justify preservation? By 1890 almost all redwood forest lands had passed from the public domain, often fraudulently, to speculators or loggers.

The main impetus to protect redwoods emerged in the 20th century and was scientific, not aesthetic. In the 1830s paleontologists had found fossils of twigs and cones resembling those of living redwoods in rock strata millions of years old. Sometimes associated with extinct animals, such fossils occurred in Europe, Asia, and North America. As a living link with the planet's newly discovered antiquity the redwood became a paleontological talisman. In 1879 Harvard botanist Asa Gray said redwoods confirmed evolution, linking the fossil past and living present.

When it became clear after World War I that the last big expanses of virgin redwoods, in Humboldt and Del Norte counties, would soon be logged, some

paleontologists launched the first national campaign for their preservation. Henry Fairfield Osborn of the American Museum of Natural History, Madison Grant of the New York Zoological Society, and John C. Merriam of the University of California at Berkeley traveled the first primitive North Coast roads to see the redwoods, publicized them, and in 1918 helped found the Save-the-Redwoods League, a private organization dedicated to buying redwood forest for preservation. Using donations and state matching funds the League bought up more than 100,000 acres of redwood forest between 1920 and 1960. Most League purchases were placed in four state parks—Humboldt, Prairie Creek, Del Norte Coast, and Jedediah Smith Redwoods state parks—stretching up the North Coast. Many people considered the redwoods saved by the four parks, along with smaller protected areas to the south, such as Big Basin Redwoods State Park and Muir Woods National Monument. From the viewpoint of early 20th-century scientists such as Merriam, the most *important* redwoods were saved, exemplars of a stage in evolution's progress upward to humanity and civilization. Their generation was less concerned to save the trees' natural setting of the Coast Range and its other plant and animal species.

The League's land purchases reflected this outlook. Most land in the four state parks consisted of the stream flats or lower slopes where the biggest redwoods grow. Madison Grant wanted to protect the watersheds above the big trees, but this proved difficult, financially and politically. Timber companies owning redwood land were reluctant to reduce their resource base. With the big trees protected, most progressives did not object to conversion of the less majestic forest of upper slopes and ridges to commercial timberland. And so the League enjoyed good relations with the business community and had great success raising money to save redwoods.

By the 1960s many conservationists were less optimistic. Science had come to place less emphasis on progress and more on stability and diversity. This outlook coincided with growing public anxiety about the future of life—human and otherwise—as environmental pollution and other side-effects of industrial growth became better known. Such anxieties led to the "environmentalist" viewpoint that we must

preserve natural ecosystems and species—regardless of their immediate commercial usefulness to civilization—to maintain a healthy biosphere. Big coast redwoods were not merely monuments to evolutionary progress, they symbolized environmental stability.

Industrial growth and redwood protection had collided at Humboldt Redwoods State Park in 1955. Logging on slopes above the park had left unstable soils exposed to erosion. Heavy winter rainfall and increased runoff from logged areas caused massive flooding on Bull Creek that swept away 500 giant redwoods and threatened thousands more by undercutting the banks and silting streams. Logging was increasing in other park watersheds, and another disastrous flood hit the region in 1964. Conservationists also were concerned when the state built a freeway through Humboldt Redwoods and planned others through Prairie Creek and Jedediah Smith; those roads were later rerouted. It seemed that 100,000 acres of stream flats and lower slopes might not be enough to save the redwoods.

The Sierra Club, which John Muir had founded in 1892, became the prime advocate for a redwood national park to include big redwoods and a sample of the entire North Coast environment, from beaches and rocky headlands to the ridgetop prairies. Approached by the Sierra Club, President John F. Kennedy's Secretary of the Interior Stewart Udall warmed to such a park. The question then was where the park would be. The Save-the-Redwoods League now supported a national park but in the Mill Creek area above Jedediah Smith and Del Norte Coast Redwoods state parks, whose fine redwood forest was also crucial watershed for the parks. Influenced by Martin Litton, travel editor of *Sunset Magazine,* the Sierra Club wanted a park on Redwood Creek, an unprotected area that in the early 1960s had an almost intact old-growth watershed. Amateur pilot Litton convinced conservationists and legislators of the area's value by flying many over it.

Redwood Creek promised the stability and diversity that the environmental viewpoint emphasized. Sierra Club ads in major newspapers stressed its range of habitats—"from groves at sea level to those at 3,000 feet"—and superior faunal, geological, and geographic variety—"the ultimate redwood wilderness." Its prestige was enhanced in 1964, when a

A split redwood along Prairie Creek reveals the heartwood source of its common name.

19

National Geographic Society survey team discovered along the creek several trees taller than any known before. This Tall Trees Grove included the tallest tree ever found, the 367.8-foot Tall Tree. Increasingly, however, redwood protection collided with industry. Local timber companies owned Redwood Creek and planned to log it. In 1964 the Sierra Club proposed a 90,000-acre park including half the creek's watershed and costing $160 million to buy from timber companies unwilling to sell. The most Congress had ever appropriated for a park up to then was $3.5 million.

Three years of ensuing political maneuvering conceded something to everybody but satisfied no one. In October 1968 Congress passed, and President Lyndon B. Johnson signed into law, legislation creating a 58,000-acre Redwood National Park consisting of Jedediah Smith, Del Norte Coast, and Prairie Creek Redwoods state parks along with some surrounding private lands (including some in the Mill Creek area), and about 20,000 acres in the Redwood Creek watershed. The $92-million park purchase saved 10,640 acres of previously unprotected old-growth redwoods, including a slender corridor of lower Redwood Creek that environmentalists disappointedly dubbed "the worm." The rest of Redwood Creek remained in timber company hands. They had been logging it since the national park was proposed and proceeded to clear cut most of the rest in the next 10 years.

It was far from the stable, diverse Redwood Creek park they envisioned, and the Sierra Club and its allies faced a potential repeat of the 1955 Bull Creek disaster. U.S. Geological Survey research revealed that eroded soils from clear-cut slopes had buried much of the original stream bed in gravel. Could not another flood roar down the creek and rip out the Tall Trees Grove? Bills to protect more land on Redwood Creek failed to pass each Congress between 1969 and 1976, however, and attempts to regulate logging along park borders also met with resistance. In 1976 Congressional hearings revealed that 90 percent of the Redwood Creek watershed had been clear cut and that the sedimentation of the creek bed was affecting "the worm."

By now both the Sierra Club and the Save-the-Redwoods League sought the purchase of the entire Redwood Creek watershed "from ridge to ridge."

The Club's book, *The Last Redwoods*, had helped to sway public opinion with its dramatic before-and-after photos of logged areas. The Carter administration favored park expansion, but two more years of political maneuvering and continued clear cutting ensued. In 1977 a well-publicized logging truck convoy went to Washington, D.C., to oppose the park and present the former peanut-farmer President with a giant redwood peanut. (Rejected by the White House, it now lies beside a gas station in Orick, just outside the park.) In 1978 Congress finally passed a bill increasing park acreage on Redwood Creek by 48,000 acres, roughly the lower third of the watershed, with an upstream "park protection zone" of another 30,000 acres in which the National Park Service would exercise some influence over logging practices on commercial timberlands. The bill also included unprecedented provisions for compensating timber workers and local communities for loss of income—because the park lands were removed from timber production—and for funding rehabilitation of the clear-cut land above the creek.

The Redwood National Park battles were among the opening salvos of the bitter conflicts over ancient forests that have torn the Pacific Northwest during the past two decades. The park since has receded from the headlines. Today the once bare clear-cut slopes above Redwood Creek are green with alders and young conifers, and park resource management staff have had some success in reducing creek siltation by removing many logging roads and skid trails. I got an idea of their success on my walk down the Dolason Prairie Trail in search of mist-hidden redwoods. The trail had been a wide logging road a few years before, but I did not realize it.

In some ways the Redwood National and State Parks come close to being the stable, diverse sample of North Coast ecosystems that environmentalists envisioned in the 1960s. These parks enable visitors to experience not only the huge river terrace redwoods of Stout, Tall Tree, and other famous groves but also a wide range of habitats. Dozens of tree and shrub species compose park forests, and there are many non-forested places. Miles of dunes and bluffs stretch along Gold Bluffs Beach. The early fall surf is sometimes bioluminescent at night, and groups of seals and sea lions play in the waves. Sea stars,

Park Expansion *Logging, timber harvest, and road building on lands that are upslope and upstream of the park boundary combined with major storms to accelerate naturally high erosion rates. Stream sediment loads increased and accumulated. Water levels were raised, and stream banks eroded. The situation threatened the redwoods and the health of the watershed.*

Conservation groups filed a series of lawsuits demanding that the Secretary of the Interior take action to protect the parklands. After lawsuits, court decisions, contentious hearings, and considerable division among local communities, Congress expanded Redwood National Park in 1978. To reduce risk of damage to downstream park resources, this legislation authorized a program to rehabilitate areas in the park and to control erosion on private lands upstream of the park.

21

anemones, and hermit crabs are plentiful in the tide pools beneath the towering headlands at Enderts Beach south of Crescent City. The bluffs and headlands are good places to watch migrating gray whales in fall and winter. Elk herds are a common sight in the meadows and prairies. River otters inhabit park streams and estuaries. At the parks' eastern extreme, on the high ridges, is another world of open spaces and long vistas.

These parks do not comprise "the ultimate redwood wilderness." With four major units divided by freeways, towns, and commercial timberlands, this scheme differs from traditional national parks such as Yellowstone or Yosemite, which encompass large uninterrupted blocks of wildland. Logging upstream on Redwood Creek and other park streams continues to cause more erosion and sedimentation. Park resource managers work closely with neighboring landowners in an effort to minimize potential impacts. The silt from pre-park logging remains in many streams, and streambeds are just beginning to regain their natural character as deep, meandering channels shaded by mature conifers. Before that, another disastrous flood could increase sediment loads. Salmon and steelhead runs will not recover until the creeks recover. Downstream, channelization and diversion in Redwood Creek's estuary also limit the stream's potential for successful spawning, because young salmon depend on living in the estuary before moving out to sea.

The parks' problems also have a useful side. Future national parks, here or abroad, may be made more in the image of Redwood than in that of Yosemite or Yellowstone, because big blocks of pristine land are disappearing. Like Redwood, future parks may be quilted together from federal, state, and private lands, rather than carved out of huge blocks of the public domain. Such parks may have to be restored as well as protected, and many of the restoration techniques learned at Redwood already are at work elsewhere in parks and on commercial timber lands. Have the redwoods been saved? The question still remains open as the debate between progress and stability continues, in the woods and elsewhere.

Roosevelt elk bulls with antlers still in velvet rest in open prairie. Elk are the parks' largest terrestrial mammals. You often see them in Elk Prairie along the Newton B. Drury Scenic Parkway in Prairie Creek Redwoods State Park, in the Gold Bluffs Beach area, in open meadows along Davison Road, or on upland prairies along Bald Hills Road in the southernmost national park area.

Part 2

North Coast Nature and Culture

The Tall Trees And the Forest

David Rains Wallace

Lush and mist-enshrouded foliage in and around redwoods along the Damnation Creek Trail masks the fact that the North Coast and New England share like latitudes. In fact the seasons are much milder here than in most of the temperate zones. The North Coast's mild climate may mainly limit redwood distribution—possibly still migrating slowly northward since the Ice Age ended. Southwest Oregon has virtually the same climate, but the coast redwood stops almost at the border between California and Oregon.

Pages 24-25: *Driftwood piles up on the sandy shore of Hidden Beach just south of False Klamath Cove and the Yurok Loop Trail.*

Pages 28-29: *Although laden with cones, a coast redwood may reproduce by sprouting as well as from seed. Either way, the tree has perhaps 2,000 years to replace itself, a handsome timespan for measuring reproductive success.*

Big redwoods can be inconspicuous, but they also can be overwhelming in the right setting. I found such a setting at midpoint on my hike from Dolason Prairie when I stood beside Redwood Creek and looked across the loosely piled, waterworn rocks of a gravel bar at the Tall Trees Grove. The morning fog had long passed, and the sunlight reflected from the green wall in the dazzling way that it reflects from highrise buildings. Redwood height can take on a transcendent aspect at such times. The green spires seemed almost metaphysical as they glowed up there with their tops at roughly the level of a skyscraper's 35th floor. Redwood height is a mysterious quality.

Despite the scientific attention the coast redwood has received, knowledge about it has grown slowly. For years after its discovery it was thought to be a kind of baldcypress, like the Spanish-moss-draped trees of southern swamps. In 1847 Austrian botanist Stephen Endlicher classified the coast redwood as a separate genus, which he named after the Cherokee leader Sequoya. Why he did so remains unclear. The giant sequoia was originally included with the coast redwood in the genus *Sequoia,* but Professor John Buchholz placed the Sierra trees in the genus *Sequoiadendron* in 1939. A third living redwood species was not scientifically discovered until 1944, when a Chinese forester noticed a specimen in a temple garden in Szechuan Province. Paleontologist Ralph Chaney, John Merriam's successor at the University of California and at the Save-the-Redwoods League, traveled to China to study it in 1948 and found small, wild populations in remote mountains there. Named *Metasequoia* or "dawn redwood," the Asian genus differs from the American ones in many ways. It is deciduous, dropping its leaves in winter, and is much smaller and shorter-lived.

Ancestral redwood fossils first appear in Manchurian, Jurassic Period rocks of about 160 million years ago, but it is not clear how *Sequoia sempervirens* de-

The dawn redwood (below) was scientifically described in Asia in 1944, and University of California paleontologist Ralph Chaney found small, wild populations of this third living redwood species in the mountains of China in 1948. Unlike the two American redwoods, Metasequoia *loses its leaves in winter. It is much shorter lived, too, and does not grow nearly as tall as these parks' coast redwood (facing page) or the Sierra Nevada's giant sequoia.*

scended from these almost unimaginably ancient trees. Many other fossil redwoods have been found throughout the northern hemisphere, and even in Greenland and Siberia. Paleontologists have thought some fossils were enough like living coast redwoods to be classed in the same genus, but others have had their doubts.

Redwoods appeared on the West Coast of North America about 20 million years ago. Before then the coastal climate had been too warm for temperate forest trees, which grew on interior plateaus. As global climate cooled and dried, redwoods migrated to the coast. Again it is not clear how West Coast fossil redwoods were related to the living species. Many have been classed in the genus *Sequoia* and seem similar to the living coast redwood. Three-million-year-old petrified logs in Sonoma County near Santa Rosa look uncannily like living redwood logs (I saw a char mark on one fossil log that might have been made a year ago), and the ancient trees were of comparable size and age. We do not know enough about the fossil trees to be sure just how they lived, however. Different kinds probably lived under different conditions, just as today's giant sequoias, at 5,000 to 7,000 feet of elevation in the snowy Sierra, have a habitat very unlike coast redwood habitat.

Fossils show that prehistoric redwoods were tall but not how they evolved that quality. Explanations for it have been speculative. Botanists have suggested that the coast redwood's tallness may be related to the fact that it is a hexaploid species, with 66 chromosomes in its cell nuclei instead of the 22 chromosomes of its relatives in the family *Taxodiaceae*. Most of these relatives, including baldcypresses and various East Asian and, surprisingly, Tasmanian conifers, are normal-sized trees. The even bigger (although shorter) giant sequoia tree is also a normally diploid species with 22 chromosomes, however.

We also do not understand how living redwoods grow so tall. A simple explanation might be that the trees just *live* long enough to reach great heights. Redwoods are unusually long-lived trees. Their wood and bark are exceptionally rich in tannin and other substances that repel the insects, fungi, and diseases that kill most trees before they live more than a few centuries. Thick and non-resinous redwood bark protects the trees from fire damage. Yet the longevity explanation of the trees' tallness has problems also. Redwoods seldom live more than 2,000 years, which is two thirds as long as giant sequoias, and only half as long as the stunted bristlecone pines on southern California mountaintops. Some very tall redwoods are very old, but others are much younger. The 362-foot Dyerville Giant, which fell in 1991, may have been 2,000 years old, but Redwood Creek's Tall Tree is only about 600 years old.

Stephen Veirs's best explanation is that some redwoods have "the genetic capacity and environmental opportunity" to grow very tall. Veirs worked many years as an ecologist in Redwood National Park. He says we do not know enough about redwood biology to say exactly what the "genetic capacity" is. We do understand enough about redwood ecology to know that the "environmental opportunity" generally consists of growing on the fertile and moist soils of the stream flats where the tallest redwoods grow. Whatever the reason for the coast redwoods' height, the species' evolutionary survival does not seem to depend on it.

Redwood reproduction is decidedly independent of size or longevity. Redwood saplings growing in the sunlight of open places can produce pollen-bearing cones 10 years after they germinate and seed-bearing cones 20 years after. Trees reproduce most vigorously during their first 250 years. Older trees produce reduced ratios of viable seeds, with as much as 80 percent of seeds empty of embryos. Coast redwoods produce a lot of seeds, but most viable seeds fail to germinate. Failure results from parasitic fungi, summer drought, or other causes.

Seedlings that germinate are very shade tolerant, however, two to four times more so than conifers such as fir and pine. Roots grow quickly and become well-developed even if trunk and branches remain stunted. Shade-stunted trees can survive for decades or even centuries on the forest floor until the fall of a canopy tree lets in the sunlight. Such "escaped" saplings, or those that have germinated in flood alluvium or other sunny spots, grow explosively. Twenty-year-old saplings can be 50 feet tall and nearly a foot in diameter.

Redwoods do not depend solely on sexual reproduction. When I was in the Tall Trees Grove I was surprised to find that the Tall Tree is actually two

Coast redwood trees can live about 2,000 years, but most live an average of 500 to 700 years. Many of the mature redwoods that have reached the forest canopy die by falling over—windthrow—or from excessive fire damage. Redwoods have no taproot, and their roots penetrate only 10 to 13 feet deep and spread 60 to 80 feet. No known killing diseases affect the trees, and they suffer no significant insect damage. Thick bark and the foliage's great distance from the forest floor help mature trees resist all but the most intense fires. Drought affects redwoods more than most other cone-bearing trees. In undisturbed forest, successful seedlings often grow in the enhanced moisture of logs or root wads of fallen trees. Redwoods also reproduce by stump sprouting, with sprouts using the toppled or burned tree stump's root system for nourishment and support. Burls at the base of a stump often sprout many saplings, and circular stands of these family groups are common. The world's tallest tree has a double trunk, and it probably sprouted from a basal burl. Tannin and related com-

*A **coast redwood tree** produces both pollen-bearing cones and ovulate cones. The pollen is shed in winter or in spring, and mature fertilized ovulate cones ripen in early autumn to shed seeds in late autumn and early winter. In forest settings redwoods produce cones only after they reach the canopy and can tap the energy of direct sunlight. A tree's tissues conduct con-*

The Redwood Tree

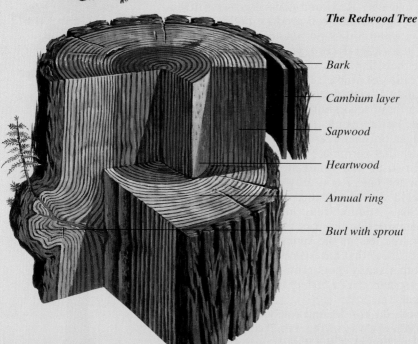

— Bark

— Cambium layer

— Sapwood

— Heartwood

— Annual ring

— Burl with sprout

pounds in its heartwood and bark give the redwood its color. Because these compounds are water soluble, where rainfall contacts the heartwood or bark they will weather to gray just as untreated redwood shingles do. Redwood forests develop the world's greatest reported volume of living matter per unit of land surface.

tinuous columns of water from roots to leaves. Water-to-water molecular bonds in the sapwood essentially drag water up the sapwood, powered by the leaves' diffusion of water into the atmosphere. On summer days redwood stems shrink slightly from the water loss. Then they swell at night as the soil moisture recharges the system.

Coast Redwood Facts

Height: to nearly 370 feet
Age: to more than 2,000 years
Bark: to 12 inches thick
Base: to 22 feet in diameter
Reproduce: by seed or sprout
Seed size: like tomato seeds
Cone size: like an olive

The Role of Fire

Fires ignited by lightning and American Indians had a great influence on natural communities before Europeans first came to California's North Coast. The managers of these parks view fire as a natural process that should function in the ecosystem whenever possible.

Old-growth Old-growth coast redwood stands developed with occasional fires that removed less fire-resistant trees, recycled nutrients, and modified vegetation near the ground. The redwood's thick bark and its ability to sprout allow it to survive and thrive even where fires regularly occur. Managers of these parks are beginning to conduct prescribed burns in old-growth stands to maintain fire's role in the natural community.

Prairies and Oak Woodlands American Indians managed the Bald Hills prairies and oak woodlands with burning to encourage production of the food and materials they needed. New

settlers continued the practice to provide forage for their sheep and to keep springs open. Now park rangers use carefully controlled prescribed burning of prairies and oak woodlands to maintain native plants, preserve wildlife habitat, and perpetuate fire as a natural process.

Range of the Redwoods

In modern times forests dominated by the coast redwood tree occupied approximately two million acres along 450 miles of coastal California and southernmost Oregon—see the large map below. Old-growth redwood forest today occupies no more than 4.5 percent (85,000 acres) of that range. The modern coast redwood species first appeared in western North America some 23 million years ago.

Other redwood species, possibly its ancestors, once were widespread in western North America.

Fossils of other species of redwood occur across the United States (including Alaska), Greenland, France, and China, and petrified forests found in Yellowstone National Park include red-wood species. While "former range" maps published over the years show redwoods once covering much of the northern hemisphere—see map at right—coast red-woods are not found in the fossil record, maybe due to recent genetic change.

Role of Fog Marine influences blanket much of the redwoods' narrow coastal range with fog. Flowing on-shore when inland temperatures are high, fog moderates

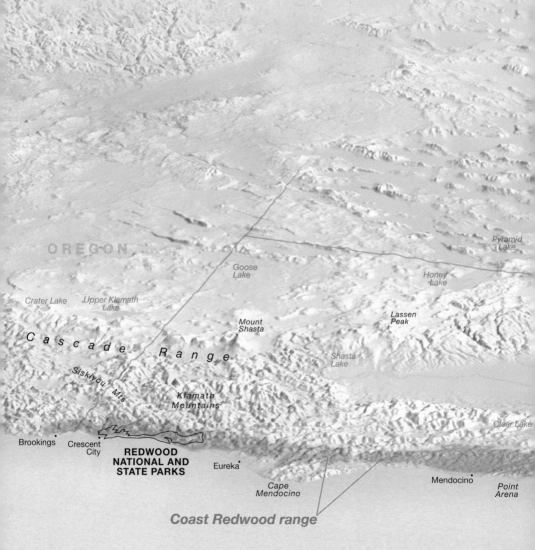

OREGON

Pyramid Lake

Goose Lake

Honey Lake

Crater Lake

Upper Klamath Lake

Mount Shasta

Lassen Peak

Cascade Range

Shasta Lake

Siskiyou Mts

Klamath Mountains

Clear Lake

Brookings

Crescent City

REDWOOD NATIONAL AND STATE PARKS

Eureka

Cape Mendocino

Mendocino

Point Arena

Coast Redwood range

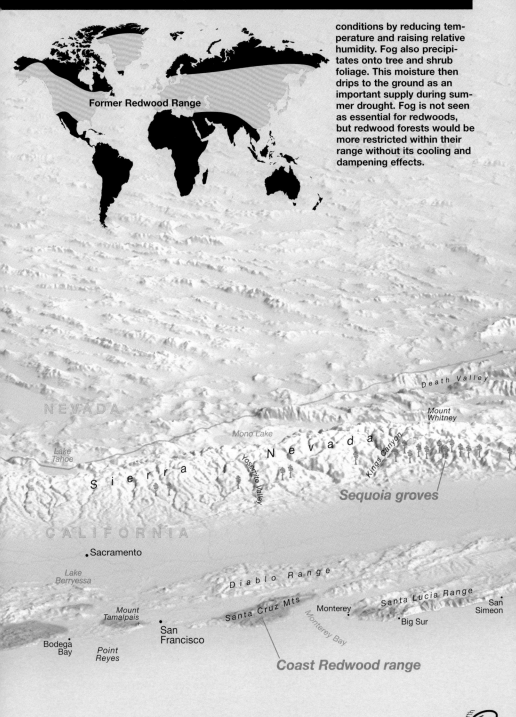

Former Redwood Range

conditions by reducing temperature and raising relative humidity. Fog also precipitates onto tree and shrub foliage. This moisture then drips to the ground as an important supply during summer drought. Fog is not seen as essential for redwoods, but redwood forests would be more restricted within their range without its cooling and dampening effects.

Death Valley

N E V A D A

Mount Whitney

Mono Lake

S i e r r a   N e v a d a

Lake Tahoe

Yosemite Valley

Kings Canyon

Sequoia groves

C A L I F O R N I A

•Sacramento

Lake Berryessa

D i a b l o   R a n g e

Santa Lucia Range

Mount Tamalpais

Monterey

San Simeon

Santa Cruz Mts

San Francisco

Monterey Bay

•Big Sur

Bodega Bay

Point Reyes

Coast Redwood range

P a c i f i c   O c e a n

North

This redwood tree was sectioned about 1985 by scientists studying the effects of a fire that occurred in 1974 (see label on page 39). The section is shown here at actual size. In its early years this tree put on wider growth rings. Later rings become more narrow. This evidence of early vigorous growth suggests that the tree grew where there was ample light available—perhaps because another fire had opened the forest canopy and allowed this tree to become established. That fire would have happened soon before 1900, just when this tree began to grow.

trees growing together like Siamese twins. The Tall Tree may have grown not from a seed but from the stump of another tree as a clone. Unlike most other conifers the coast redwood can grow new stems from basal burls when trunk and branches are cut, burned, or broken off. Redwood burls are gnarled structures that form from axillary buds on seedling redwoods and grow larger as the tree matures. They become masses that ring the base of the trunk or sometimes form clumps farther up the trunk. The burls are made up of many small, dormant stems covered by bark. When cutting or other damage removes the main trunk's biochemical dominance, these dormant stems start growing. They can grow even faster than sexually reproduced seedlings, because they get water and nutrients from the existing root system. Eventually a few of the stems may grow into giant trees genetically identical to the original tree. The Tall Tree and its twin may have started as such burl sprouts (although they also may have grown from two seeds that happened to sprout close together).

Redwood non-sexual reproduction raises the possibility that so-called "genetic individuals" could live for a number of generations as their basal burls and root systems continually grow new trees after old ones are killed. The life span of a coast redwood might thus be many times the 2,000 years that is generally the maximum for individual trunks. As yet, botanists have been unable to document an example of such a redwood clone, but the Tall Tree may be a much more venerable organism than its 600 annual growth rings would suggest.

The coast redwood is such a vigorous species that its relatively confined range, about 450 miles by 25 miles, and below 3,000 feet of altitude, can seem surprising. Planted redwoods thrive around the world, but the species' natural reproduction appears specialized for northern California's coastal climate, a fairly unusual one by present global standards. (It may have been much more widespread in the past.) Redwood foliage wilts in high temperatures and may be killed by hard frost, so the North Coast's mild climate is probably the main limiting factor on the species' distribution.

Large redwoods daily transpire hundreds of gallons of water vapor into the air through their foliage, about twice a household of three's average water

● Growth ring about 1904

use. The North Coast's abundant rainfall, to 122 inches annually, is thus another factor. Redwood reproduction coincides with the October-to-May rainy season. Pollination occurs from November to February, and the cones open and shed their seeds at the end of the following summer. Reproduction is usually more successful in rainy years than dry ones.

Coastal fogs help to protect the redwoods from drought and heat during the stressful summer. The fogs form above upwellings of deep and cold ocean waters, then move inland, drawn by hot air rising in the interior. "Fog drip" from water vapor condensing on treetop foliage often renders the forest floor soggy even after months without rain. Redwoods do not need fog to survive, but fog reduces the stress of rainless summers. In some parts of the range, stands grow in interior canyons where coastal fogs seldom occur. Still, the most impressive redwood forest coincides with regular summer fogs and higher rainfall.

Yet present climate does not entirely explain redwood distribution. Southwest Oregon has virtually the same climate as northwest California, but the coast redwood stops almost at the state line—as though abetting the rivalry between these states. Stephen Veirs thinks redwood range "may have expanded northward in the last 10,000 years," which could mean that the species is still migrating north in response to warming climate since the Ice Age ended. The coast redwood may eventually range farther north, given another 10,000 years.

The coast redwood does not grow everywhere even within its range. Despite its common name, the species is not tolerant of salty air, and seldom directly faces the ocean. Strong shoreline winds also discourage redwoods, because the foliage dries out easily and is killed by salt spray.

Clearings caused by fire, logging, or road building also can damage adjacent forest through desiccation and windthrow. Sometime after its discovery in 1963, the top of the Tall Tree, the world's tallest tree, began slowly to die back. Subsequently, dense new foliage has regrown near the top of the tree, but the highest point is now a dead spike, probably resulting from exposure caused by human modification of lands around Tall Trees Grove. The second tallest tree has not suffered such die-back and may be the record holder now. Redwoods respond to harsher condi-

Thick bark helps protect the redwood from fire.

Burn scars about 1974

39

tions at treetop levels by producing pale green, awl-like needles quite different from the lush, dark green needle sprays of their shaded branches. On windy days park trails often are littered with branchlets of this foliage blown down from the treetops.

Charred bark on most big redwood trees shows that forest fire was widespread before modern times, although the frequency of such fires is uncertain. Summer lightning fires used to spread unchecked for days and even weeks before modern foresters began to suppress them. The thick-barked, old-growth redwoods are highly fire-resistant, particularly in moist flood plains and on lower slopes, but smaller redwoods and those that grow on higher slopes are less so. The increasing scarcity of big redwoods as one moves upslope and inland is thus probably a result of fire as well as the drier and hotter local climate. Large fires can kill even big redwoods, and fire may have been the main cause of redwood mortality under primeval conditions.

Redwoods grow on a variety of soil and rock types. They do best on moist alluvial land but also reach impressive size on the slopes of shady gorges. Most of the redwood's range is underlain by the rocks of the Franciscan Formation, a melange of sandstone, schist, and other sedimentary and metamorphic rocks that was deposited under the Pacific about 100 million years ago and has since been uplifted by movements of the Earth's crust. These rocks also predominate in the parks. There are geological substrates where redwoods do not thrive. Like many other plants, redwoods are absent from the greenish serpentine bedrock and reddish soils of the Little Bald Hills adjacent to Jedediah Smith Redwoods State Park, perhaps because the rock's chemical composition is toxic to them. On the steep ridges of the Bald Hills redwood forest gives way to grasslands and oak woodlands. Tree seedlings able to become established on the unstable clay soils there usually succumb to grass fires before attaining much size.

Factors that limit coast redwoods are ecological opportunities for other tree species. They are sometimes the redwood's helpers, sometimes its rivals. On my walk from Dolason Prairie to Redwood Creek, the beauty of the other plants impressed me as much as the redwoods, although some were harder to identify. But that added to the forest's fascination. "A per-

Tanoak A hardwood, the tanoak grows well beneath the high redwood canopy, where its seedlings tolerate shade more than redwood and western hemlock seedlings do. Tanoak acorns establish themselves in forest floor duff better than the seeds of most trees.

Western hemlock Smallest of the important lumber trees, the western hemlock averages 150 feet tall but can grow 250 feet tall. Its seeds often sprout on fallen logs called nursery logs because of this. Its thin bark makes this tree susceptible to fire and fungi.

Douglas fir A monarch of North Coast mists, the Douglas fir can rival redwoods for height. The Douglas fir typically grows farther inland and at higher elevations, but their ranges can overlap, so the Douglas fir and redwood are sometimes seen growing in the same area.

Western redcedar Growing at the southern limit of its range in these parks, the western redcedar does not reach the heights it does in the Pacific Northwest. There it played the role in American Indian material culture that the redwood plays here on the North Coast.

fumed and purple light lay in the pale green of the underbrush," wrote novelist John Steinbeck of a redwood stand. "Gooseberry bushes and blackberries and tall ferns . . . met and cut off the sky."

Structural diversity distinguishes redwood forest as much as grandeur. Although the North Coast forest, with a dry summer season, is not really temperate rainforest like that of the Olympic Peninsula, where rain falls year-round, it can stand beside the finest temperate rainforest in the vibrancy and variety of its life. Like rainforest it has a five-tiered structure with an upper story of giant redwoods, a canopy of smaller but still huge conifers, a subcanopy of hardwoods, and then shrub and herb levels near the forest floor.

Douglas fir is the major tree of the coniferous canopy beneath the big redwoods. It grows everywhere redwoods do, from the valleys to the highest ridges. Adapted to germinate best on bare, exposed sites, it is most common in drier, hotter, more frequently burned areas. The Douglas fir can reach a height of far more than 300 feet in old growth, making it the world's fourth tallest tree species (after an Australian eucalyptus species and the giant sequoia).

On the shore prickly-needled Sitka spruce outcompetes salt-sensitive redwood to form almost unbroken stands. These spruce stands buffer the redwoods from salt and wind. Spruce trunks can get as broad as medium-sized redwoods but are readily identified by the jigsaw-like pattern of their bark. Spruce grows inland on the boggy soils of coastal valley bottoms but disappears on drier slopes. Western hemlock is another important conifer of moist forest sites in the parks. As shade tolerant as redwood, its seedlings often grow on fallen logs, sending long roots down to the ground. Hemlock occurs farther inland than spruce.

Grand fir is less common than spruce and hemlock but grows throughout these parklands. Several other coniferous species occur more locally. Western redcedar, at its southernmost range here, is found occasionally in moist coastal areas. Its fluted bark is like the redwood's, but its lacy foliage is different. A related, lacy-foliaged tree, Port Orford cedar, grows along streams in the very different environment of the Little Bald Hills.

Hardwoods are as ecologically important as the conifers, and none is more important than red alder, the silvery-barked relative of birch now covering the clear cuts of the national park. Alder is a pioneer tree that colonizes disturbed ground. Through nitrogen-fixing bacteria in its roots it enriches the soil but gives way to more long-lived species that eventually overtop it, shading it out. Willows and cottonwoods also grow along streams and help to stabilize banks. On older stream flats bigleaf maple and evergreen California laurel form hardwood groves like that on the edge of the Tall Trees Grove. California laurel, or bay, also grows in the shade of mature conifers, along with tanoak. An evergreen with glossy, serrated leaves, tanoak is as shade tolerant as the redwood. Madrone is a less common but distinctive subcanopy tree found more often on hot, dry slopes. It has fast-shedding bark that can be dark red, bright orange, or beryl green according to the time of year.

The shrubs are even more diverse than the trees. Just listing those with the word *berry* in their name suggests this: blackberry, black huckleberry, coffee-berry, elderberry, gooseberry, osoberry, red huckle-berry, salmonberry, snowberry, thimbleberry, and twinberry. The most magnificent shrub is the rose-purple-flowered California rhododendron so wide-spread on slopes and river terraces. It grows to 20 feet tall. Its pink-and-orange-flowered relative west-ern azalea occurs in the Little Bald Hills and other sites on the parks' eastern margins.

Considering the forest's shady masses of trees and shrubs, it is impressive how many herbaceous plants grow on its floor, many more species than its woody plants. Spring wildflowers are the most spectacular of these—such as one colony of pink calypso orchids I found where the redwoods emerged from the fog on the Dolason Prairie Trail. But lush greenery abounds throughout the year from perennial herbs such as redwood sorrel as well as grasses, ferns, club mosses, liverworts, and mosses. Fern Canyon in Prairie Creek Redwoods State Park, its walls covered with five-fin-ger, deer, lady, and other fern species, is a rightfully famous example of such abundance.

The forest floor is the most complicated and least understood part of the forest. Most plants depend for health on symbiotic relationships, called mycor-rhizae, with fungi that grow in or on their roots. The

fungi live on food produced by the plants and in return help the roots to absorb water and nutrients from the soil. Some plants cannot grow without them. And the thousands of fungus species interact in turn with thousands of other soil organisms from burrowing rodents to protozoa and bacteria.

Perhaps some of the answers to the mysteries of redwood height and longevity lie in the forest floor, in ancient partnerships between the greatest living things and the humblest. Scientific studies in the 1980s showed that old-growth temperate coniferous forests such as those in Redwood National and State Parks have some of the highest known diversities of soil organisms in the world. For example, a hundred fungus species have been counted on the roots of the Douglas fir tree.

Much of what we know about old-growth forest has been learned even since Redwood National Park was established. People used to think that old growth was a "biological desert" with less plant and animal diversity than younger forest. These parks' quiet groves may give the impression that few animals live here. But recent research has shown that a diverse group of animals depends wholly or partly on old growth for survival. Some use the forest in unexpected ways: that marbled murrelets nest in redwood canopy was not discovered until the 1970s. Many are uncommon, like spotted owls, or only present seasonally, like salmon. Many are abundant but small and secretive, like the red tree voles that also build nests high in the redwoods. There is much, much more to be learned about such things, as there is about the redwood itself.

Ancient redwood forest old growth is a supreme example of forest evolution as well as tree evolution. It is "ancient forest" in every sense of the term. As the forest's senior member the coast redwood is far from being an archaic relic ready for the museum. Compared to most organisms, indeed, the redwood is an ultimate survivor. While dinosaurs, mastodons, and many human civilizations have come and gone, it has remained—adapted to occupy its present coastal habitat indefinitely but also quite capable of adapting to change.

By their sharp contrast, these stands of Oregon white oaks define the baldness of Bald Hills upland prairies above Redwood Creek valley. The rich mosaic of diverse habitats protected within these Redwood National and State Parks is increasingly important for a number of rare and endangered plant and animal species.

Disturbances — And Restoration

Malinee Crapsey

From the tiny poundings of raindrops to the huge scour of ocean waves, this landscape knows well the changes wrought by water. It is intimate with the wind that topples trees, creating openings in its forest mantle. From its highest prairies to its wettest woods, fire has burned holes in the evergreen canopy. Disruption by natural forces makes these redwood parks a patchwork of the quick and the dead. Whatever loses its life—to wind or flood or fire—is resurrected as the yet-living take advantage of the space vacated or the nutrients released. This circle of life has perpetuated itself here since long before humans first walked these shores.

Eons of evolution, however, never prepared this ecosystem for many of the ways we humans have disturbed it in modern times. Logging, and even more so the extensive road-building that accompanied it, challenge this landscape and those who caretake it to absorb or deflect disturbance on a new scale. These parks now embrace a rich mosaic of lands whose response to disruptions, both natural and human-caused, is at the heart of both their natural glory and their management challenges.

The dramatic Pacific Ocean shoreline comes as a surprise, lying as it does within the boundaries of a place named only for its trees. While it is the wind that makes waves, the waves must get the credit for molding this stunning intersection of land and sea. As they wash over the leading edge of the continent waves erode it not only by water action but also by scouring every surface with sand. Waves even push a pillow of air in front of them, and compressed into cracks it can blow particles from the rock.

Life should be hard put to find a foothold here, but in fact the rocks are carpeted with it. In the belt between the highest and lowest tides myriad life forms cling to the rocks tenaciously—and ingeniously. Familiar from restaurant menus, California mussels attach themselves with filaments stronger than

49

At low tide small creeks may cross the beach as broad ribbons of water on an uncarved streambed of sands newly rearranged by each high tide. Rock outcroppings characteristic of these parks' coastal scenery bear the brunt of violent storm waves.

Below: *Gray whales pass near shore here on their yearly migrations between Alaska's Bering Sea and Mexico's Baja California. By the late 1940s whaling had all but wiped out California gray whales. Their population slowly rebounded once they were listed under the Endangered Species Act in 1970. In 1994 the gray whale was de-listed, removed from the Endangered Species List.*

steel threads. More strange are flower-like anemones whose emerald green echoes the verdant plantlife inland. These relatives of the jellyfish glue themselves directly to rock. Many times I have seen children approach these bizarre lifeforms emboldened by a stick. The truth is, little in the tidepools can hurt you, unless you fall on barnacle-coated rocks or turn your back on the waves. One such child who chose to trust me abandoned his stick and took to stroking a giant green anemone. What won his affection? I think it was the knowledge that this soft creature, armored only with pebbles stuck to its skin, might be 100 years old.

Some species keep moving, albeit slowly. Limpets and chitons, cousins to the snails, slide about when high tides cover them but batten down during tidal changes, their smooth surfaces deflecting the power of crashing waves. Predatory sea stars do the same. Snails, not as flat or smooth, slide into cracks as far as they can to avoid being washed away when the waves start rushing in. Other animals take advantage of the excellent connections made by the colonies of mussels, anemones, and algae growing cheek by jowl; soft, slender sea worms, insect-like isopods, and even tiny fish moor themselves under and between these living anchors when the seas get rough.

Between rocky points curve softer beaches, their sand the pulverized faces of the bluffs above and sediment carried to the sea by rivers. Here there is no solid rock to hang onto. Life must tunnel below the sandy layers that shift and scour with each wave. Using very different types of feet burrowers such as Pacific razor clams and mole crabs dig down out of harm's way—and our view. Prodding beach rubble is not for the squeamish, but this is where you find evidence of the losers in these encounters with the sea's awesome energy. Crab carcasses and broken shells litter the edge of the last tide's highest reach. Yet the clumps of rotting seaweed ripped from the ocean floor by heavy seas always evoke for me the long-abandoned theory of spontaneous generation, the notion that life could arise, without parentage, in piles of just such refuse. Lift the unappealing mass, and well-fed kelp flies, sand fleas, and other little amphipods suddenly appear, leaping about your feet.

Just above the intertidal zone, where those without gills feel more at ease, is a strip of land shaped more by fresh water. Subsurface water seeping through ocean-facing ledges and bluffs causes earth to slip and slump toward the beach. Heading over, across, and below some of the landslides lying along these parks' coastal trails has left me contemplating the chances of a very personal encounter with erosion.

Paths carved by rivers and creeks through such varying coastal landforms are themselves varied: narrow gorges like Fern Canyon, the spreading delta of the Klamath River, and marshy estuaries like the mouth of Redwood Creek. The waterways deliver to the ocean whatever debris they have the energy to carry, from fine sediment to, during floods, enormous inland trees. These behemoth trunks lie placidly on the beach in summer, but I have watched winter waves hurl them like battering rams against the shore, further testing life's hold there. As they approach the ocean rivers develop split personalities. Salt water combines with fresh. Flow continues seaward, yet high tides slow it down and push ocean water deep into the streams' throats. This mix is an estuary, the aquatic interface between the land and ocean. Estuaries provide nurseries for young salmon and steelhead. Born in the rivers, these anadromous fish pause to grow here before adopting their sea-going lifestyle and heading into the rigors of the open ocean. Wave action makes the estuary such a safe place. As flows decrease in smaller rivers in summer, waves will nearly seal off the stream mouth by building up a berm, a dam of sand and silt that the river is too weak to break. For weeks then the river backs up, spreading out over the low land of its delta, creating even more habitat for young fish and other life. Eventually the river overwhelms and breaches the berm, and the juvenile fish can move out to sea.

What wave wash does to rocky headlands, fire does to prairies. By sweeping the environment regularly, it creates conditions in which certain types of life flourish. Early residents learned to mimic the effects of lightning fires. Local Indians burned to make acorn collection easier under the oaks, to clear land, and to stimulate the growth of food for game. The ranchers who came later did the same. For more than a century, however, we have feared the use of fire as an agent of change and for the most part suppressed it. By the late 1960s attentive observers were recognizing our mistake. By staying the hand of natural dis-

Treasures of the Coast

How would you like to spend two six-hour shifts per day under water and also face the risk of crushing wave shock in ocean storms? Nature asks just this of tidepool creatures. Remarkably a North Coast tidepool (below) may boast more diversity of life than the lush redwood forests do. Visibly zoned the ecological niches in tidepools are more readily recognized than those in forests. Along the some 33 miles of Pacific Coast these parks protect, winds push the warmer top layer of ocean water offshore and create the fog that helps to water the redwood trees. And the winds feed coastal marine animals: as winds move warmer water offshore, nutrient-rich waters well up from the depths. One sea-land connection that was unknown until recently concerns an endangered species. The marbled murrelet, a sea bird, nests in the upper canopy of redwoods and makes forays to sea for food for its young. California gray whales that migrate along the coast

in spring and fall occasionally beach. In the past a beached whale might feed one North Coast Indian village for half a winter season. Park naturalists lead activities (photo at left) to help you get to know firsthand these treasures of the coast.

A western trillium beckons potential pollinators against a backdrop of Oxalis, or wood sorrel.

Opposite: *A reflective and serene freshwater pond on Lagoon Creek gives little indication of how close its waters are to joining Pacific surf. Lying right along U.S. 101 the Lagoon Creek area makes a handy spot to watch both native and migrating birds. Nearby are the Lagoon Creek picnic area and Yurok Loop Trail, a self-guiding trail that connects with the Coastal Trail.*

turbance we were losing whole landscapes and the wildlife that depends on them. These prairies, wonderful open spaces that crown the hilltops above Redwood Creek and the Smith River, were shrinking. Liberated from fire some Douglas fir trees were shouldering their way into the openings and shading out the grass favored by elk and deer for forage. Fire is returning to these prairies now. Planning the burn's timing, intensity, and size, park managers use it to kill off young firs and alien grass species that threaten to take over. Lightning stands ready to reclaim its natural role in resetting the clock of growth here once we cease thinking of it only as an arsonist.

Fire also pays infrequent but important visits to redwood forests, opening space for new life to get a start. I saw its marks in the big trees of Prairie Creek Redwoods, Jedediah Smith Redwoods, and Del Norte Coast Redwoods state parks. In the Redwood Creek drainage of the national park, however, I was almost completely distracted by other disturbances—caused by us. I work in national parks and believe in the values of preservation, so it was disconcerting to discover a park purposefully created to *include* clear cuts. When the national park first joined the older state parks in 1968 our usual preservation tool, a park boundary, would not suffice to save the big trees. The effects of earlier human activities outside the new park swept across the boundary into its protected forests, causing damage, unintentionally.

It was the fall of 1959. This was a deep, narrow drainage then, one of many clefts in the hillside carrying water towards Redwood Creek: The man on the bulldozer was in a hurry to build a road across the creek to the forest scheduled to be cut before the seasonal rains came. He started to build another "Humboldt" stream crossing by working his bulldozer carefully to lay five large logs in the steep creek so the water still flowed beneath the logs. Then he cut out the hillside and dozed a thick layer of earth over them to create the roadbed. Building the crossing took a lot of skill and the best part of a day, maneuvering the dozer on the steep forested slopes.

With any luck the stream would flow between the buried logs and not wash out the road bed—at least until the timber cut was completed. When the buried logs couldn't channel rainwater fast enough it would

Streams of Salmon and Steelhead

Salmon possess uncanny homing ability. After three or four years at sea they return to the stream of their birth and spawn in gravels there. How? No one knows for sure. Chinook (king) and coho (silver) salmon and steelhead—called anadromous species, from the Greek for "running upwards"—ascend from the sea to breed in these parks' Klamath and Smith rivers and Redwood Creek. Steelhead are sea-run rainbow trout. Salmon and steelhead stockpile ocean nutrients—they eat Pacific fish and shellfish (including shrimp and crabs)—and periodically carry these resources inland in the form of fish flesh. North Coast Indians depended on these spawning runs for important dietary protein. So did bears, eagles, and the many other animals that lined banks or plunged into the streams to gorge on the living fish or spawned-out carcasses. Salmon run on Redwood Creek from late November to early January; steelhead from early January to mid-March. Fall-run salmon move up the Klamath River in mid-July. The spring run of chinook begins in early March. Indian groups used elaborate safe-

King (Chinook) Salmon

Silver (Coho) Salmon

guards to assure continuing supplies of these fish—and sea-run sturgeon, lampreys, and cutthroat trout—both for themselves and others upstream. Today, salmon still is important for ceremonial and subsistence use. Now modern over-fishing, streams silted up by erosion, and other factors threaten many spawning runs, greatly diminished compared with historic times.

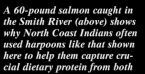

A 60-pound salmon caught in the Smith River (above) shows why North Coast Indians often used harpoons like that shown here to help them capture crucial dietary protein from both rivers and the Pacific Ocean. In the large photo, an Indian uses a dip net to harvest small fish.

pool up in the drainage behind the road that was now turned into a dam blocking the stream's normal flow.

It seemed that the rains of December 1964 would never stop, although local folks knew they'd seen worse in '55 and surely would again. Still, the warm rain coming in on top of the snow made the runoff extra heavy that year. And high on the steep slopes of the Redwood Creek watershed water pooled behind the crossing on the now-abandoned road and then began to overflow. Commanded by gravity it sought the easiest way downhill and followed the small roadside ditch for a ways. Hitting a tangle of branches and leaves the little flood spilled out onto the road and then meandered down until it crossed to the downhill side. Now completely diverted from its natural drainage the stream began to carve a new channel for itself down the steep hillslope where previously there had been no channel.

Some 3,000 cubic yards of soil eroded because of that stream crossing alone. The gully it carved where it dropped off the road grew to 10 feet deep, 15 feet wide, and 500 feet long. The water carried its burden of earth downhill to the next stream it encountered. The heavy load of sediment-laden water sluiced into that channel, overloading its own delicate equilibrium. It cut deeply into its banks, eroding them and adding more to its sediment load. A chain reaction was created, washing tons of sediment that eventually washed into Redwood Creek upstream from the Tall Trees Grove.

This was by no means a unique event. Hundreds of drainages were crossed by logging roads and skid trails. Water and gravity overcame human engineering and sent thousands of tons of dirt into Redwood Creek. The creek bed was buried an average of eight feet deep as a result of this single storm. This sediment, moved slowly by the current at a rate of less than one-half mile each year, may take decades to wash out to sea. And as this wave of sediment moves downstream the resulting flooding, erosion, and sedimentation kills successive stretches of riverbank trees or undermines them, causing them to topple. This destruction of forest and stream has dealt a heavy blow to the salmon and trout once abundant in Redwood Creek. The threat of damage to the Tall Trees Grove and other spectacular groves along Redwood Creek convinced Congress in 1978 to

An Indian harpoon (below) hints that big fish lurked in the parks' rivers and coastal waters. Some do still.

Opposite: *The South and Middle forks of the Smith River flow together just outside Jedediah Smith Redwoods State Park. Not far downstream, foot trails in Stout Grove lead briefly along the river bank and through the grove's oldgrowth redwood forest.*

Few parks can boast such a great seashore-to-mountains wealth of animals and plants that calls these parks home. Gray whales cruise offshore, seals and sea lions haul out on the offshore rocks or on shore, seaweed kelp forests exceed redwood forests in biological diversity, tidepools and splash zones host myriad forms of life in neat layers, rivers and creeks channel the spawning salmon and trout inland, old-growth redwood forest harbors threatened and

Bloodstar

Harbor seal pup

Banana slugs

River otter

endangered species, and grassy prairie uplands are dotted with acorn-producing oak and tanoak trees. Roosevelt elk, black bears, black-tailed deer, and mountain lions are present in healthy populations. Managers of these parks work to maintain and restore the environment's biodiversity, its number and relative abundance of species native to the North Coast's Mediterranean climate. Preserving its biodiversity also preserves both natural processes and genetic diversity—with who knows what other values in the future? This area boasts more than 350 native species of birds.

California sea lions

Douglas squirrel or chickaree

Mink

Northern spotted owl

Mountain lion or cougar

Dipper or water ouzel

expand the park upstream and upslope. Thus 48,000 logged acres with 300 miles of roads became part of a national park. In an extraordinary move Congress directed the National Park Service to restore these lands and to reduce the erosion caused by logging.

Almost two decades later I visited Redwood Creek near the Tall Trees Grove. I did not realize that I was walking on as much as 10 feet of sediment that suffocated the roots of some upstream redwoods as the sediment slug passed them in the late 1970s. Many shallow streams criss-crossed warm, barren gravel bars. Old photographs show a deep single stream in its narrow bed with conifers on both sides reaching across and shading the creek's entire width in places.

In other rivers I have seen salmon so immense they reminded me of these redwoods, beautiful old veterans of countless natural battles. These impressive fish will spawn in Redwood Creek and its tributaries, given the right habitat. Now, however, the clean gravels they dig their nests in are covered with silt; few eggs get enough oxygen to hatch. Of those that do some of the young will be choked by sediments. Sediment has filled in many of the deep, cool pools fish prefer. Streamside trees that used to shade the creek were swept away as the channel broadened, so that now sunlight heats the water to temperatures unhealthy for these fish. Between these changes and the unnatural disruption of the creek's estuary, we are severely testing the ability of salmon and steelhead to survive in Redwood Creek. Now the summer steelhead runs are down to but a few dozen fish.

With the 1978 addition to Redwood National Park, Congress decreed that the new, logged park land would be restored in order to slow erosion. Enter geologist Terry Spreiter, member of a team of talented individuals dedicated to the task: "When I started work here in 1980, I was assigned the Dolason Creek watershed and told to figure out how to fix it. But most erosion control techniques back then had been developed for use on flat agricultural land. We experimented with a lot of new ideas. We thought planting trees would stabilize roadfills and hold the sediment in place." Even deep-rooted trees, however, were no match for gravity acting on as much as 20 feet of saturated road fill. "At first we were reluctant to use heavy equipment, since big equipment had caused all the damage," Terry says, but the limitations quickly became apparent. "Now we're using the same sort of equipment that built the roads to take them out—and sometimes the same people."

Jay Franke is one of those "same people." He grew up working weekends in his father's old-growth redwood mill and started running bulldozers—they call them "Cats"—on logging roads after high school. The mill closed in 1977. "We might've lasted a few years longer if the national park hadn't been created," Jay said, "but eventually all the old growth would be gone anyway." Five years later Jay contracted to work removing roads in the national park. "I looked at what they were trying to do and said, 'Now how're you going to do all this with that little tiny equipment?' I brought a big, good-running Cat up to the park, and people were impressed by the amount of dirt it could move. It took time for me to learn what the park people wanted and for them to learn what I could do. We needed to learn what should be done—we're still learning, looking at earlier work as it weathers. This is something that's never been done before."

Now the big machines take the stream crossings apart before they fail, pushing fill out of the drainages and putting it back into the road cuts. As they dig down to uncover the natural stream channel, they often find old tree stumps buried in the fill. These serve as good guides to the profile of the original land surface. The original topsoil is often uncovered and laid back in place over the filled-in road. Long-dormant seeds in that topsoil often sprout, helping to revegetate the scars of the logging work.

"We didn't pay that much attention to what we were doing," Jay says of his former road-building years, "we just did it as cheap as we could. If it went in the stream, it went in the stream. Those old roads are the ones causing the problems. Now, I think people are more conscious about what they do. Timber companies really don't want to see their lands wash away. And the laws have changed. When I started on one project in the '70s, I suddenly wasn't allowed to shove anything over the edge—which I thought was strange at the time. But in '89 we built three miles of road for a timber company, and they did a really good job keeping water in its natural drainages and sediment out of the creeks."

Prairies and Roosevelt Elk

Named for President Theodore Roosevelt, Roosevelt elk are both native to these parks and their largest mammals. They are commonly seen in meadows along U.S. 101, at Elk Prairie along Newton B. Drury Scenic Parkway, and in the Gold Bluffs Beach area. Roosevelt elk favor prairies for their grasses and grass-like plants and especially favor the rapid new growth of shrubs and saplings that follows logging or other landscape disturbances. Indians routinely set fires to make the land more productive—and to attract the elk, thousands of which also lived in oak-dotted prairies of the Bald Hills (photo at right) in the early to mid-1800s. Male or bull elk grow antlers yearly, shedding them after the fall mating season or rut, when cow elk form harem groups. By summer's end a mature bull's six-point rack may weigh nearly 40 pounds. One male will dominate the harem, with bachelor bulls banding together in a separate group. Bulls bugle often during the rut. Females bear their spotted calves in late spring or early summer and

then form female-dominated herds that may include year-ling males. Older bulls may live alone or will form small bands and replenish weight loss from rigors of the rut. Do not approach elk closely. The bulls are fiercely protective of cows, as are cows of calves. Any apparent lack of concern about your presence does *not* mean elk are tame.

Restoring Redwood Creek's Watershed

In 1978 Congress added 48,000 acres to Redwood National Park and directed the National Park Service to rehabilitate the logged-over lands to slow down the erosion. Some 36,000 acres of upslope clear cuts poured silt and debris into Redwood Creek—which threatened to topple the world's tallest trees and to obliterate salmon and trout spawning habitat. The restoration work goes on, and this task includes removing more than 300 miles of logging truck haul roads and 3,000 miles of log-skidding trails (see inset photo at right). Searching for permanent, mainte-nance-free solutions, the National Park Service learned to use bulldozers like those that had built the haul roads and skid trails to put back nature's original landscape. Old profiles of hillsides and

stream channels are re-contoured to restore conditions favoring the return of natural vegetation. Where revegetation might be slow, workers plant coast redwood and Douglas fir seedlings to reconstitute the natural ecosystem mosaic.

In 1982 this logging road (photo at left) was recontoured, the culvert removed, and the natural stream channel uncovered (middle photo). By 1987 vegetation (photo at right) had all but obscured the fact that a road once crossed this landscape.

I recently visited a stretch of logging road—near Rodgers Peak—that was removed in 1988. Tramping along a broad, level road cut into the forested hill-slope, I was not prepared for what I saw: a pile of rocky rubble and then no road. The contour of the slope looked completely natural, and a swath of healthy young shrubs and conifer seedlings ran on through the woods. "Roads have a psychological permanence," Terry observed. "They're all around us, and we depend on them to take us wherever we go. You never see a road disappear out in the real world. When we started the rehabilitation work, we set our sights too low. We just didn't believe we could really get rid of a road. But we learned we can."

More than 170 miles of such roads have disappeared in the park portion of the Redwood Creek basin, but Jay stated it matter of factly: "There are still a lot of old roads out there just waiting to fail." Not all are on park lands. Park geologists now work with park neighbors, mostly timber companies and ranches, to rehabilitate the roads on private lands upstream. Geologist Greg Bundros directs this program. He has found that all the major commercial landowners are willing to cooperate in this work.

The next challenge is second-growth forests. Most of the logged land added to the national park in 1978 is in varying stages of regrowth. Much of this is "dog hair," as the dense stands of skinny trees are called. "We're just starting to grapple with how to improve the most accessible stands to promote aesthetics and wildlife, to advance it toward the old-growth characteristics," Terry says. "The second growth is like a reserve for the future. A hundred years from now the human population will be bigger. We'll need more trails. It's like having park land in the bank."

This dedication to understanding natural systems and restoring them is cause for optimism. So are the combined federal, state, and private efforts to preserve and restore the landscape. Despite all the apparent setbacks, the natural and human-caused changes evident in these parks, these places seem steeped in immortality. There is a sense of timelessness to the waves pounding on the shore. In the golden grasses of the prairies history feels present and alive. The redwoods, too, rising skyward through their moist, jade forest, inspire a certain sense of permanence. Endurance in the face of change.

On foggy mornings you can often rise above lack of clarity—by standing with Oregon white oaks on the Bald Hills. Here, seen from Schoolhouse Prairie, the marine-influence fog separates you from but does not obscure the great redwood forests standing far below along Redwood Creek.

Healing the Land And Ourselves

Ed Zahniser

Fanny Meldon Flounder, a Yurok doctor, practiced her basket maker's art. Basket making meshes the practical, artistic, and spiritual—and reveals how intimately California's North Coast Indians inhabit a world saturated with spirit, story, and society.

What would it feel like to be part of a world whose plants, animals, rocks, and mountains were members of your family? The Constitution of the Yurok Tribe reflects this world view:

"Our people have always lived on this sacred and wondrous land along the Pacific Coast and inland on the Klamath River, since the Spirit People, *Wo-ge'* made things ready for us and the Creator, *Ko-won-no-ekc-on Ne-ka-nup-ceo,* placed us here. From the beginning, we have followed all the laws of the Creator, which became the whole fabric of our tribal sovereignty. In times past and now Yurok people bless the deep river, the tall redwood trees, the rocks, the mounds, and the trails. We pray for the health of all the animals, and prudently harvest and manage the great salmon runs and herds of deer and elk. We never waste and use every bit of the salmon, deer, elk, sturgeon, eels, seaweed, mussels, candlefish, otters, sea lions, seals, whales, and other ocean and river animals. We also have practiced our stewardship of the land in the prairies and forests through controlled burns that improve wildlife habitat and enhance the health and growth of the tan oak acorns, hazelnuts, pepperwood nuts, berries, grasses and bushes, all of which are used and provide materials for baskets, fabrics, and utensils.

"For millennia our religion and sovereignty have been pervasive throughout all of our traditional villages. Our intricate way of life requires the use of the sweathouse, extensive spiritual training, and sacrifice. Until recently there was little crime, because Yurok law is firm and requires full compensation to the family whenever there is an injury or insult. If there is not agreement as to the settlement, a mediator would resolve the dispute. Our Indian doctors, *Keg-ae,* have cared for our people and treated them when they became ill. In times of difficulty village headmen gather together to resolve problems affecting the Yurok Tribe."

Shuttles were used in making and repairing fishing nets for use in rivers and coastal waters.

Yurok ancestral lands occupy the majority of Redwood National and State Parks. Other ancestral lands in this area include those of the Tolowa and Chilula Indians. Loren Bommelyn, Tolowa tribal council member, basket maker, and story teller, echoes the spirit the Yurok express when he says that "Redwood is at the heart of our existence and life."

Bommelyn is a certified teacher of the Tolowa language. He does not use the definite article *the* before the tree, just as you or I would not say "the Richard" of a friend. That only makes it more compelling when Bommelyn explains that "In our linguistic view of the world there is not a clear separation between animate and inanimate." Only Tolowa language fleshes out the stories of the Tolowa people. Nevertheless Bommelyn explains how "Redwood is at the heart of Tolowa theology." "We have been here since the time of origins." "Trees, salmon, canoes were our buffalo, our mainstay of life." "In killing a tree to make a canoe one understands that the spirit of the tree remains in the canoe when you put it in the water." "If you can fall a redwood tree you can fall any tree in the world. Each one falls uniquely. They are individuals and are like humans in that respect." All of life could be said to be a way of seeing the trees.

It is difficult to put ourselves in the mindset of the earliest European explorers here and thereby grasp how they might have perceived what were to them unknown lands. This North Coast could well have seemed forbidding as seen from shipboard, with its 300-foot treeline of dark forests draped in dense fog.

In 1775 Spanish ships anchored at the village of Tsurai (pronounced *chur-aye*), in what we now know as Trinidad Bay. They transported an expedition meant to cement Spanish claims against those being pressed down northern California by Britain's ambitious Hudson's Bay Company to the north. Shortly after 1800 sea otter furs would draw American, Russian, and British ships to the North Coast, but the otters were quickly depleted, and interest waned.

We know from journals of Spanish explorers that Indians living in this area had metal implements by 1775. The journals of Jedediah Smith also noted this fact in 1828. Smith had reached California's northern coast by traveling overland from the east. The fact suggested to Smith and his party that the Indians in this area had links to Hudson's Bay Company trade to the north. But the Indians had long before found metal in the remains of shipwrecks washed ashore.

No doubt metal implements and other trade goods brought changes in how the Indians lived here, but sudden, massive change began for them about 1848. The treaty of Guadalupe Hidalgo in that year ended the Mexican-American War. With the treaty the United States received nearly half of Mexico's total territory, including what is now California. This was the first treaty involving the Indians of northwestern California. Today the treaty of Guadalupe Hidalgo remains vitally important to them, because it guaranteed rights for the Indians.

This United States takeover of California coincided with the gold rush, which struck the North Coast about 1850. A rapid influx of gold-seeking adventurers overwhelmed and displaced Indian groups and denied them access to their traditional food sources. Unfamiliar and deadly diseases, starvation, and outright conflict combined to decimate Indian residents thoughout the area.

"The initial contact was gruesome," Malcolm Margolin writes in *Living in a Well-Ordered World: Indian People of Northwestern California.* "The newcomers simply pushed the Indians off their land, hunted them down like animals, scorned, raped, and enslaved them. Resistance—and many of the Indians did resist—was often met with massacres."

Gold also was found in 1850 as dust layers lying on the Gold Bluffs Beach area of today's parks. Those high bluffs are ancient outwash sediments deposited by the ancestral Klamath River that had delivered the gold from inland hills. (The mouth of today's Klamath River lies to the north.) The population of Trinidad, which was founded by commercial interests, ballooned, but few people got rich mining. Many more people got rich running pack trains and other services to supply the needs of the miners. It proved too difficult to separate the gold and the sand, and this costly effort negated any would-be mining profits. The Union Gold Bluff Placer Mine made money in the late 1870s and early 1880s, but it fared poorly in the 1890s and ceased operations in 1902.

The enduring "color"—as the mineral prospectors called economic promise—was not gold but redwood. Given redwood's top-market lumber values and appeal today, it is wrenching to recall that the

The Tolowa, Yurok, and Chilula Indians historically controlled lands now included in Redwood National and State Parks. Chilula Indians were later assimilated into the inland Hupa culture.

Four native cultures have ties to these parks and continue to make their homes on the North Coast—the Tolowa, Yurok, Chilula, and Hupa. Archeological records reach back here more than 6,000 years, and today's Indians carry on traditional ceremonies, arts, and subsistence skills. When people who had European backgrounds first visited here these Indians enjoyed high population densities and complex cultures. The Redwood Coast Indians cultivated the land's productivity with timely burning, pruning, weeding, and planting. Centuries of adapting to living in California had taught them sophisticated land-use practices that differed from European practices. Managing the landscape by burning enhanced plant and animal resources, and especially the protein-rich acorn crops. Burning also helped maintain complex plant associations and the animal life depending on such diversity. Burning improved animal forage and

Baskets are of many types, and some serve very specific purposes. These are Tolowa baskets, except for the wider, Yurok gathering basket.

browse. It was management of game by herding and attraction. Sophisticated legal systems combined with ritual to enable these peoples to manage sustainable harvests of the seasonal salmon and steelhead runs. At the coast they took seals, sea lions, shellfish, and the occasional beached whale. They also foraged nutritious seaweeds and gathered shorebird eggs. Indians used redwood for houses, sweathouses, and canoes. Planks for buildings were split off using elk antler wedges and stone mauls. Storm or lightning-felled redwoods were used for canoes, some more than 40 feet long. Much travel was by river.

Longer, sturdier ocean-going canoes were used for seal hunting, offshore fishing, and coastal travel. Canoe makers chose their trees carefully so the craft would not split.

North Coast Indian houses are made of redwood planks. The Yurok house (above) is located at Patrick's Point State Park. Polly Albert (left) was a Tolowa basket maker.

trees were first cut commercially here for making boxes. Nor were these today's artisan-worked collectibles but *boxes:* packing boxes, bread boxes to be shipped to Alaska, Central America, Hawaii, Australia, Tahiti.

At first, logging redwoods meant hard labor by hand with huge crosscut saws their wielders called "misery whips." At the rate at which one redwood could be cut down and bucked up for transport to a sawmill then—dragged by oxen over skid roads or loaded onto wagons—the supply of trees may have seemed endless. But by the time Loren Bommelyn's father worked the woods industrial-era logging with mammoth chainsaws, bulldozers, railroads, and, later, heavy trucks rapidly made short work of what redwood trees still remained. Demand for lumber burgeoned worldwide after World War II as the bombed out cities of Europe and Japan were rebuilt and new U.S. prosperity plus five years of pent-up demand for housing created what John G. Mitchell described as "an orgy of homebuilding." *Today, more than 95 percent of all old-growth redwood forest has been cut down.*

There have been other attempts to come to economic terms with nature here. Area Indians caught the ocean-fed salmon that ran up coastal waterways from time immemorial. Elaborate cultural patterns regulated how many salmon could be caught—so that supplies of the fish would be adequate both over the generations and up and down these watersheds. Commercial salmon fishing began here in the early 1880s at the Klamath River mouth. One early venture featured a light-draft steamboat from Gold Beach, Oregon, as a floating cannery. Upset at this intrusion the Yurok who traditionally fished at that location joined a Crescent City entrepreneur to supply a competing cannery at Requa.

Markets farther and farther away determined how many salmon were caught: the living rituals developed over untold generations of Indian experience no longer enforced their crucial ecological restraint.

Traditional homelands of the Tolowa, Yurok, and Chilula Indian groups make up today's national and state parks. Traditional homelands of Hupa Indians lay southeast of today's parks, encompassing the lower Trinity River. In the old days Indians throughout this region lived in villages along major rivers

Amanda Carroll, Yurok, holds a doll basket made by her grandmother Patricia Hunsucker. When the photograph was taken Amanda was a beginning basket maker.

Gold Rush and Gold Bluffs

Gold strikes in 1848 on the upper Trinity River precipitated a rush to the North Coast of California. California's population grew four-fold from 1850 to 1860. Here the boom proved even more dramatic. Trading companies founded Trinidad and Eureka in 1850, and Eureka boasted 3,000 people by 1853 when miners founded Crescent City. These coastal towns served as supply centers. Goods brought by boats from San Francisco went inland on mules to supply miners. Contact between gold-seekers and the North Coast Indians was sudden and, for the latter, devastating. In fewer than 20 years, decimated by armed conflict, massacres, and the new diseases, most of the remaining Indians lived on reservations. In 1850 gold was discovered at the Gold Bluffs Beach area of what is now Prairie Creek Redwoods State Park (large photo). The gold lay in black sands that big storm waves occasionally washed from the high bluffs, which are ancient Klamath River sediments. (Today's wide sandy beaches did not exist then, and storm waves sometimes struck the bluffs.) Early tries at collecting this fine gold were not productive, but strong gold prices during the Civil War fueled renewed mining at the

Gold Bluffs. The best years for profits came in the 1870s and 1880s (inset). The most gold recovered in one year brought $37,000.

Theo Howatt filed saws for a timber company. He stretched out on this redwood plank in 1884 to show off its size.

Opposite: *In the early days of their logging redwoods were cut by workers using double-bitted axes and 12-foot cross-cut saws. Wedges driven into the saw cut forced the tree to fall. Log lengths were split by blasting. Even so it took eight to 12 oxen to drag the chunks out of the woods.*

and the coast. Their squarish houses were wooden, with pitched roofs. They were built over pits dug out to about 12 feet per side. Many native people believe some of these houses date back to the time before humans lived on the Earth. Because it was Spirit Beings who first lived in them, these redwood-plank houses can be as integral to the more-than-human world as the mountains, rivers, and redwood.

Even within the relatively small area that makes up today's Redwood National and State Parks, Indian groups could be very distinct, and they spoke different languages. (California as a whole hosted some 80 to 100 languages when non-Indian settlers first arrived.) Traveling in California in 1870 Stephen Powers complained that "a new language has to be looked to every 10 miles sometimes." Cultures may have merged somewhat, but languages maintained their distinctiveness. Of the six traditional languages in this region three were of Athabaskan language family origin, two of Algonkian, and one of Hokan. Tolowa, Yurok, Hupa, and Karuk remain living languages spoken by a few tribal members, as Tolowa is both spoken and taught by Loren Bommelyn.

Indeed, language can tell us a great deal about how a given culture sees the details of its world. The literal meaning of the Yurok word for salmon, for example, *nepu,* is "that which is eaten." For the Yurok, in other words, *salmon* and *food* are synonymous.

As the enumeration of species in the Preamble to the Yurok Constitution makes clear, fish were varied and abundant. They once crowded this region's clean rivers and its great reaches of ocean coast. Over the course of many centuries North Coast Indians developed a range of techniques and implements to tap this abundance for food. In addition to using harpoons and fishhooks the Indians trapped fish with communally erected fish dams and basketry traps and netted them with ingenious bag nets, plunge nets, and drift nets, as well as fishing from their redwood dugout canoes.

Fishing remains centrally important to Indians throughout northwestern California not only for economic reasons but for cultural and spiritual reasons. "Salmon are God's gift to the Yurok," says a Yurok fisherman who lives at the Klamath River's mouth. He expresses his people's belief that their rights to fish have their origin in the very beginnings of time.

Logging the Redwoods

Commercial logging began soon after 1850, at first ignoring redwoods because early mills could not handle such big logs. A sawmill went up at Crescent City in 1853 near Third and C Streets almost as the city was platted. Soon the properties of redwood created markets for its lumber. The head chopper oversaw felling the big trees with double-bitted axes and 12-foot-long crosscut saws operated with an assistant—until power saws came into use in the 1930s. Choppers made the undercut with axes, but the wedges driven into the saw's cut forced the tree over. A poorly felled redwood could shatter thousands of board feet of lumber. Teams of eight to 12 oxen dragged lengths of log, halved or quartered by blasting, out of the woods. In 1882 John Dolbeer developed the steam donkey engine. It pulled logs to roads and coupled them for the ox team. In 1892 the bull donkey was developed. It gradually replaced the oxen—its powerful engine had cables up to five miles long and could skid trains of 10 logs. In 1916 highleading was developed to drag the logs suspended from cables rigged to spar trees topped

150 feet up for the purpose. Railroads (large photo) eventually brought logs out of the woods, crossing valleys on wooden trestles (left). When logging boomed after World War II, bulldozers cut roads and skidded logs for loading on trucks that hauled them to the mills.

Despite this fact the Indians have had to struggle for many decades for their right to avail themselves of that gift. Their adversaries are not only the demands of commercial and sports fishing interests but the environmental degradation and pollution of many of the rivers and streams of their traditional tribal lands.

No land animal loomed larger for its usefulness to Indian peoples than the deer. In former times deer provided food, skins for clothing and blankets, bones for awls, and brains for use in tanning leather. Deer provided materials for many other uses as well. They still remain an important source of food for many Indians today. In the old days the deer were either snared or stalked. Snares strung across known deer trails caught deer that often were driven into them. In stalking deer with a bow and arrow the hunter, wearing a stuffed deerhead mask, often pantomimed the animals with such finesse they mistook him for another deer. And this was only after the hunter first carefully prepared himself for the hunt by bathing and then rubbing himself down with fragrant herbs to disguise his human scent.

It was not in redwood forests themselves that deer and other wildlife were plentiful, however. It was surrounding areas that once abounded with the great herds of elk that fed in meadows and with mountain lions that preyed on deer. Bald eagles, coyotes, and bobcats were also common. Open areas were especially crucial as habitat for both the elk and deer that Indians so relied on then. Grassy meadows were so valuable, in fact, that the Indians maintained them as open areas by periodically setting fire to them.

Sometimes the past comes back and begs explanation. Sometimes it offers one: land stewardship concerns of Indian groups and the federal and state parks managers today are cycling back toward common ground. Resource managers are now experimenting with prescribed burning in these parks' old-growth redwood forests, and they now use fire to restore historic conditions of prairies and to enhance their biological diversity. Decades of fire suppression have altered the landscape, allowing coniferous trees to encroach on the prairies.

Indians used fire to maintain open, park-like landscapes. Formal studies of Indian ethnography and stories told or recorded by early travelers agree in attesting that great portions of the landscape were then open grassland. As we have seen, to describe these Indians' relation to the land as "food gathering" betrays a cultural bias. They were essentially pursuing agricultural practices, not only fire management but loosening the soil and thinning tuberous plants both to harvest some and to encourage the growth of others. These practices went unrecognized as agricultural techniques in the experience of many early observers whose concepts came exclusively from European farming.

Bill Beat is a former district superintendent for the North Coast Redwoods District of the California State Parks System. He sees the methods we now use to care for the landscape more closely tracking the traditional Indian methods.

"You have to realize that those people were here for easily 5,000 years and managed to leave a much lighter footprint on the land than we have in 200 years," Beat says. "So just from that standpoint, you have to listen to what they say."

Today's natural resource management turns out to have been yesterday's cultural resource management. Our newest, developing methods of caring for the land now approach how the Indians traditionally understood the dynamics of such stewardship. Now the openness of the prairies and oak woodlands of the Bald Hills is once again maintained through the use of fire. Yet from the traditional perspective of the Indians we must preserve not only the physical environment but the spiritual environment.

Newton B. Drury's career advocating protection for redwoods included heading up the Save-the-Redwoods League. In the 1920s Drury led the League's successful campaign for legislation authorizing state parks for California. Drury also led land acquisitions for California's State Park Commission, headed California's State Division of Beaches and Parks, and served as director of the National Park Service.

The fourth child of Jonathan and Amelia Lyons was born at the couple's ranch in the Bald Hills in 1870. Jonathan Lyons had come west over the Oregon Trail at age 19, in the gold rush days. Eventually he settled on sheep ranching on the ridge-covering prairies in what is now the southernmost area of the national park. Lyons had first made his living in this region by supplying the miners and prospectors. "A mule was his market," was what Lyons's obituary in 1913 said of his early years. Working as a butcher then Lyons hawked his meat from mining camp to mining camp, sides of beef slung on his steady mules. Later on Lyons raised mules for the packing trade, which continued into the 1900s in this region. And then he switched to raising cows and horses before finally starting to raise sheep.

Fever-pitch demand for redwood lumber in the housing boom after World War II brought urgency to saving redwoods. The 1950s saw redwoods logged off at three times any previous rate. "It was clear," historian Susan Schrepfer wrote, "that the old-growth redwoods were endangered . . . . Even those redwoods in state parks were threatened by erosion and freeway construction." Since 1918 the Save-the-Redwoods League had been raising the funds to buy redwood lands. Its efforts would help create the California State Parks System. League-donated lands form the core of Prairie Creek Redwoods, Del Norte Coast Redwoods, and Jedediah Smith Redwoods state

The private, nonprofit Save-the-Redwoods League, founded in 1918, early advocated protecting the tall trees and, as its seal (left) proclaims, does so today. The League began raising funds to buy redwood forest lands and was instrumental in the establishment of California's system of state parks beginning in the 1920s.

The Sierra Club, founded by John Muir in 1892, also fought for decades to see redwood forests protected. Stewart L. Udall, secretary of the U.S. Department of the Interior for Presidents John F. Kennedy and Lyndon B. Johnson, heard these conservationists' alarm. Udall helped make Redwood National Park a reality.

parks. They were the nuclei of Redwood National Park as created in 1968. Redwood National Park was novel because it combined state and federal lands and was motivated by ecological concerns. Saving exemplary redwood trees on stream flats at the base of privately owned watersheds did not work, however. In 1978 Congress expanded the park by some 48,000 acres—8,990 were of old-growth redwood, 2,000-plus of oak woodlands and prairies, and some 37,000 of cutover lands, mostly clear cut. Congress also directed the National Park Service to restore those damaged lands and mandated a protective zone on non-park lands of the watershed. Today there are no large complete watersheds containing redwood trees protected anywhere. Lady Bird Johnson and former President Lyndon B. Johnson (far right) stand behind President Richard M. Nixon at the ceremony dedicating the national park in 1969. They are in the grove named in her honor above Little Lost Man Creek.

Lyon's wife Amelia was a Hupa Indian. Her tribe's traditional homelands encompass a portion of the drainage of the Trinity River southeast of the Bald Hills, which separate the Trinity and Klamath rivers from Redwood Creek in today's national park. By 1876 the Lyons family—Josephine, the only girl among their seven children, was born that year—were ensconced as sheep ranchers in the Bald Hills. Perhaps it was Amelia or one of the many Indians the couple regularly employed in their ranching operations who taught Jonathan Lyons to burn the Bald Hills prairies to keep them open and to increase the nutrient value of the forage they would provide for livestock. Eventually the Lyons family ranched 8,000 acres in four units in their sheep operation. You can visit one of their nicely refurbished barns a short walk below the Bald Hills Road.

Uncannily the spiritual environment announces itself along the Bald Hills Road up near where the Lyons family raised its sheep for several generations. Indian sites cluster along a rocky ridge here, sites whose use goes back at least 4,500 years. From such heights not far from these parks' highest point atop Schoolhouse Peak, expansive vistas sweep down off the prairies dotted with Oregon white oaks, and down to the stately coniferous forests below the fog level, down and down into the marine climate regime where redwood monarchs endure.

What *does* it feel like to be part of a world whose plants and animals and even the rocks and mountains are members of your family?

Perhaps the question is best answered by Yurok elder Minnie Macomber. She recommends that visitors to this area follow another old-time custom: "Sometimes we would just sit someplace, maybe by a pool or where the trees are beautiful. Just sit and think good thoughts. That's enough."

Several species of ferns growing up its steep walls give to narrow Fern Canyon both its name and its magic.

Next pages: *Two generations share an enlarging sense of our human smallness within the majestic Stout Grove in Jedediah Smith Redwoods State Park.p*

Part 3

Guide and Adviser

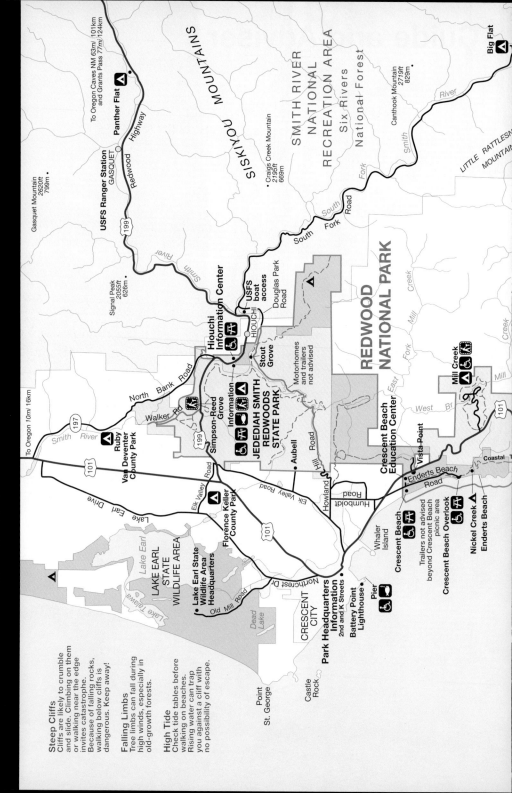

Steep Cliffs
Cliffs are likely to crumble and slide. Climbing on them or walking near the edge invites catastrophe. Because of falling rocks, walking below cliffs is dangerous. Keep away!

Falling Limbs
Tree limbs can fall during high winds, especially in old-growth forests.

High Tide
Check tide tables before walking on beaches. Rising water can trap you against a cliff with no possibility of escape.

To Oregon 10mi/16km

Point St. George

Castle Rock

CRESCENT CITY

Park Headquarters Information
2nd and K Streets

Battery Point Lighthouse

Pier

Whaler Island

Crescent Beach

Trailers not advised beyond Crescent Beach picnic area

Crescent Beach Overlook

Nickel Creek

Enderts Beach

Enderts Beach Road

Coastal

Dead Lake

Old Mill Road

Northcrest Dr.

Lake Earl State Wildlife Area Headquarters

LAKE EARL STATE WILDLIFE AREA

Lake Earl

Lake Talawa

Florence Keller County Park

Elk Valley Road

Elk Valley Road

Humboldt Road

Howland Hill Road

Lake Earl Drive

Smith River

Ruby Van Deventer County Park

To Oregon

197

101

101

REDWOOD NATIONAL PARK

JEDEDIAH SMITH REDWOODS STATE PARK

Information

Simpson-Reed Grove

Walker Rd

North Bank Road

199

Aubell

Hill Road

Crescent Beach Education Center

Vista Point

Mill Creek

Mill Creek

West Br.

East Fork Mill Creek

Creek

Motorhomes and trailers not advised

Stout Grove

Hiouchi Information Center

HIOUCHI

USFS boat access

Douglas Park Road

Signal Peak 2055ft 626m

Smith River

199

Redwood Highway

GASQUET

USFS Ranger Station

Panther Flat

To Oregon Caves NM 63mi/101km Grants Pass 77mi/124km

Gasquet Mountain 2620ft 799m

SISKIYOU MOUNTAINS

Craigs Creek Mountain 2195ft 669m

South Fork

South Fork Road

SMITH RIVER NATIONAL RECREATION AREA

Six Rivers National Forest

Smith River

Canthook Mountain 2719ft 829m

Big Flat

River

LITTLE RATTLESN MOUNTAIN

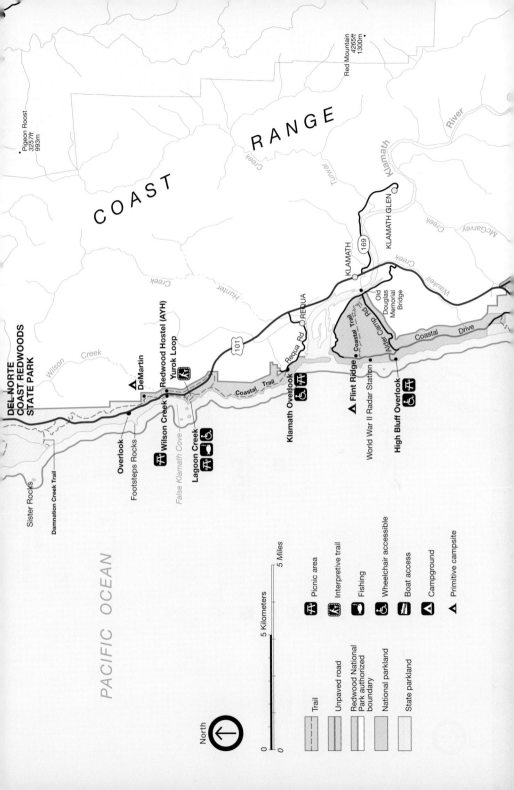

COAST RANGE

Red Mountain
4265ft
1300m

Pigeon Roost
3257ft
993m

Klamath River

Tuwaı

Klamath

KLAMATH GLEN

169

KLAMATH

McGarvey Creek

Waukell Creek

Creek

Creek

Creek

Hunter

REQUA

Requa Rd

101

REQUA

Coastal Trail

Old Douglas
Memorial
Bridge

Alder Camp Rd

Coastal Trail

Flint Ridge

World War II Radar Station

Coastal Drive

DEL NORTE
COAST REDWOODS
STATE PARK

Wilson Creek

DeMartin

Redwood Hostel (AYH)
Yurok Loop

Overlook

Footsteps Rocks

Wilson Creek

Lagoon Creek

Coastal Trail

Klamath Overlook

High Bluff Overlook

False Klamath Cove

Sister Rocks

Damnation Creek Trail

PACIFIC OCEAN

North

5 Kilometers

5 Miles

Picnic area

Interpretive trail

Fishing

Wheelchair accessible

Boat access

Campground

Primitive campsite

Trail

Unpaved road

Redwood National
Park authorized
boundary

National parkland

State parkland

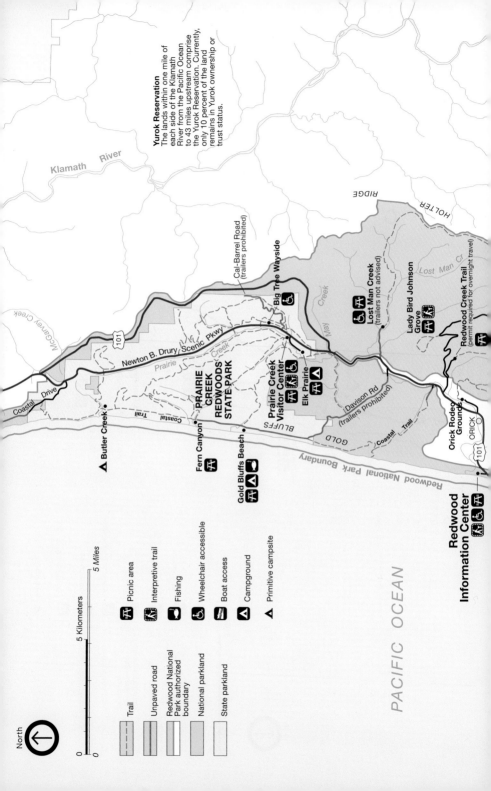

Yurok Reservation
The lands within one mile of each side of the Klamath River from the Pacific Ocean to 43 miles upstream comprise the Yurok Reservation. Currently, only 10 percent of the land remains in Yurok ownership or trust status.

Klamath River

McGarvey Creek

HOLTER RIDGE

Cal-Barrel Road
(trailers prohibited)

Big Tree Wayside

Lost Man Creek
(trailers not advised)

Lost Man Cr

Newton B. Drury Scenic Pkwy

101

Prairie Creek

PRAIRIE CREEK REDWOODS STATE PARK

Lady Bird Johnson Grove

Redwood Creek Trail
(permit required for overnight travel)

Coastal Drive

Fern Canyon

Prairie Creek Visitor Center

Elk Prairie

May Creek

Davison Rd
(trailers prohibited)

Gold Bluffs Beach

▲ Butler Creek

Coastal Trail

Trail

BLUFFS

GOLD

Coastal Trail

Redwood National Park Boundary

Orick Rodeo Grounds

ORICK

101

Redwood Information Center

PACIFIC OCEAN

North

0   5 Kilometers
0   5 Miles

Trail

Unpaved road

Redwood National Park authorized boundary

National parkland

State parkland

🍴 Picnic area

📷 Interpretive trail

🎣 Fishing

♿ Wheelchair accessible

🛶 Boat access

⛺ Campground

▲ Primitive campsite

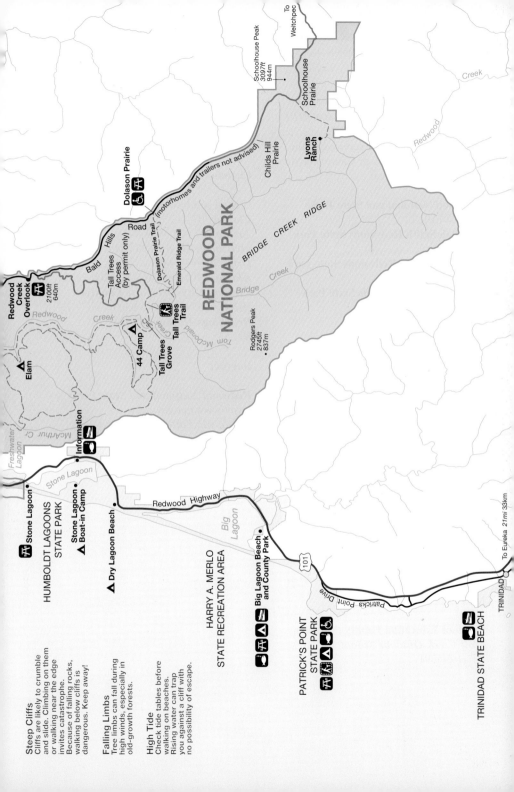

REDWOOD NATIONAL PARK

To Weitchpec

Schoolhouse Peak
3097ft
944m

Schoolhouse Prairie

Redwood Creek

Lyons Ranch

Childs Hill Prairie

Dolason Prairie

Bald Hills Road

(motorhomes and trailers not advised)

Dolason Prairie Trail

Emerald Ridge Trail

Tall Trees Access (by permit only)

Redwood Creek Overlook
2100ft
640m

Redwood Creek

BRIDGE CREEK RIDGE

Bridge Creek

Rodgers Peak
2745ft
837m

Tom McDonald Creek

Tall Trees Grove

Tall Trees Trail

44 Camp

Elam

McArthur Cr

Freshwater Lagoon

Information

Stone Lagoon

HUMBOLDT LAGOONS STATE PARK

Stone Lagoon

Stone Lagoon Boat-in Camp

Dry Lagoon Beach

Redwood Highway

Big Lagoon

HARRY A. MERLO STATE RECREATION AREA

Big Lagoon Beach and County Park

101

Patricks Point Drive

PATRICK'S POINT STATE PARK

TRINIDAD

TRINIDAD STATE BEACH

To Eureka 21mi 33km

Steep Cliffs
Cliffs are likely to crumble and slide. Climbing on them or walking near the edge invites catastrophe. Because of falling rocks, walking below cliffs is dangerous. Keep away!

Falling Limbs
Tree limbs can fall during high winds, especially in old-growth forests.

High Tide
Check tide tables before walking on beaches. Rising water can trap you against a cliff with no possibility of escape.

Phone Numbers

Emergency 911

General Parks Number: 707-464-6101
The voice mail menu lets you choose park information and visitor services, or the National Park Service or California State Parks business offices.

Redwood National and State Parks
707-464-6101
Jedediah Smith Redwoods State Park
707-465-2142
Del Norte Coast Redwoods State Park
707-465-2146
Prairie Creek Redwoods State Park
707-488-2171

Campground Reservations
800-444-7275

Redwood Information Center
707-465-7765
Crescent City Information Center
707-465-7306
Jedediah Smith Visitor Center
707-465-2144
Prairie Creek Visitor Center
707-465-7354
Hiouchi Information Center
707-458-3294

Redwood Park Association
Mail Orders 707-465-7325
North Coast Redwood Interpretive Association
Mail Orders 707-488-2169

Outdoor Education Facility (Summer)
Wolf Creek Outdoor School
707-465-7391

Highway Conditions 800-427-7623

Concessioner

Redwood Hostel 707-482-8265

Chambers of Commerce

(Listed south to north)
Eureka 707-442-3738, 800-356-6381
Arcata 707-822-3619
McKinleyville 707-839-2449
Orick 707-488-2885
Klamath 707-482-7165, 800-200-2335
Crescent City-Del Norte County
707-464-3174, 800-343-8300
Brookings-Harbor 541-469-3181,
800-535-9469

Internet

Redwood National and State Parks
http://www.nps.gov/redw/
California State Parks
http://www.parks.ca.gov

Approaching the Parks

Are you visiting Redwood National and State Parks by car, truck, or other private vehicle? If so, be aware that it is entirely possible to drive completely through these parks and not realize you have been in or close to some of the world's most magnificent forests and tallest trees.

If your itinerary is tight, you may lack time to backtrack to see the many wonders of these parks. Orienting yourself with the maps of the parks in this handbook will help prevent disappointment:

If you are traveling from the south, stop first at the Redwood Information Center. There you can ask about turning east on the Bald Hills Road to see lovely grasslands and the Tall Trees Grove in this southern portion of the national park. From Bald Hills Road you can scan these parks' most sweeping vistas of old-growth redwoods (often with the ocean as backdrop), enjoy the open uplands prairie that contributes the baldness to the Bald Hills name, view elk, examine historic structures of the sheep-ranching era, and much more.

As you drive farther north back on U.S. 101, be sure to turn onto the Newton B. Drury Scenic Parkway. This takes you through Prairie Creek Redwoods State Park with its Prairie Creek Visitor Center, Elk Prairie, elk herds, and many miles of trails.

If you are traveling from the north via U.S. 199, stop at the Hiouchi Information Center to orient yourself to Jedediah Smith Redwoods State Park before you drive on to Crescent City.

If you are traveling from the north via U.S. 101, stop at the Crescent City Information Center at Second and K streets in downtown Crescent City. Ask there for explicit directions for taking the Howland Hill Road loop *back* to Stout Grove in Jedediah Smith Redwoods State Park. Also ask about stopping at Crescent and/or Enderts beaches and also taking the side road to Mill Creek in Del Norte Coast Redwoods State Park. Such side trips introduce you to the stupendous meetings of mountains, sea coast, and ancient redwood forests that characterize Redwood National and State Parks.

U.S. 101 traverses or skirts Redwood National and State Parks from near Orick on the south to just a few miles shy of the California-Oregon boundary. Along this ribbon of highway, tops of silvered redwood snags rise above the thick second-growth forest, outlining for us all the shape of an ancient forest gone to fulfill our needs and desires. Now-vacant air, once

Western azalea

97

crowded with treetops, shows the huge size of our demands.

For most of this route U.S. 101 is dual- or four-lane highway. Other roads in these parks vary from scenic parkways to steep, winding, sometimes narrow gravel roads on which trailers and motorhomes are not advised or are restricted or prohibited.

Always pull safely off the road surface at a designated turnout or parking area to enjoy the scenery or watch wildlife.

Though many desire the experience you cannot drive through a tree in these red-wood parks. One famous drive-through tree was not a redwood but a giant se-quoia named the Wawona Tree. A cousin to these parks' coast redwood trees it grew in Yosemite National Park, south of here and far inland of the coast redwood's range. The Wawona Tree toppled in 1969.

Three redwood trees you can drive through are commercial ventures near Redwood National and State Parks: Klam-ath Tour-Through Tree near Klamath, Shrine Drive-Thru Tree near the town of Myers Flat, and Chandelier Tree in Leggett. Fees are charged.

Drive Safely Take your time and enjoy your visit. Speed limits are posted for your safety. Watch for wildlife, rocks, changes in the road surface from slides and road slumping, tree branches, and slow-moving traffic. Be alert for logging trucks and other heavy vehicles. If traffic backs up behind your car, use a turnout and let faster traffic pass. Fog is common here; drive slowly and carefully during inclement weather and use your head-lights. Rain is common November through March and can make pavement slippery.

For your protection Always lock your unattended car. Lock all valuables out of sight in the trunk or carry them with you.

Gasoline Gasoline and other supplies and services are available at communities along the highways through these parks.

Public Transportation

Scheduled airlines serve the Eureka-Arcata Airport in McKinleyville, 28 miles south of the Redwood Information Cen-ter. Cars may be rented there. Commuter flights serve the Crescent City airport— limited car rentals. Greyhound buses serve the North Coast.

Some tour companies may make stops in Redwood National and State Parks, but transportation throughout the parks is almost exclusively by personal vehicle. Once in the parks, however, you can take advantage of the foot, horse, and bicycle trails for more intimate experiences. The parks boast more than 200 miles of trails for exploring a variety of habitats from old-growth redwood groves and other woodlands to grasslands and seashore.

Trillium

Why Redwood National and State Parks? California's Department of Parks and Recreation and the National Park Service cooperate in managing three state parks and the national park to protect magnificent ancient coast redwood trees and their environment. The parks include mountains and more than 30 miles of Pacific Ocean coast. Congress established Redwood National Park in 1968 and expanded it in 1978 to augment the protection of redwoods and to link these state parks— Jedediah Smith Redwoods State Park, Del Norte Coast Redwoods State Park, and Prairie Creek Redwoods State Park—that California established in the 1920s.

A Biosphere Reserve and World Heritage Site Together the Redwood National and State Parks are a World Heritage Site. They are also part of the California Coast Ranges Biosphere Reserve. These international treaty designations serve to enhance the protection of superlative natural and cultural resources worldwide. The Man and the Biosphere Program fosters harmonious relations between humans and the biosphere through domestic and international cooperation in interdisciplinary research, education, and information exchanges. World Heritage Site designation confirms the exceptional universal value of places that deserve protection for the benefit of all humanity and other species, too.

Redwood National and State Parks provide five information centers. Information centers exist to help you make the most of your time in these parks and to help you understand the area's nature and culture. Rangers there can answer your questions and help you tailor activities to your itinerary, interests, and ambition. A variety of exhibits and audio-visual programs provided at information centers introduce the parks and important features of area environments.

Redwood Information Center, one mile south of Orick on U.S. 101, open daily, year-round, 9 a.m. to 5 p.m. Closed January 1, Thanksgiving, and December 25.

Prairie Creek Visitor Center, six miles north of Orick on Newton B. Drury Scenic Parkway, open daily, summer 9 a.m. to 5 p.m., winter 10 a.m. to 2 p.m. Closed January 1, Thanksgiving, and December 25.

Crescent City Information Center, 2nd and K Streets, Crescent City, open daily, year-round, 9 a.m. to 5 p.m. Closed January 1, Thanksgiving, and December 25.

Hiouchi Information Center, 10 miles northeast of Crescent City off U.S. 199, open daily in summer only, 9 a.m. to 5 p.m.

Jedediah Smith Visitor Center, open daily in summer 9 a.m. to 5 p.m., in winter as staffing allows. Closed January 1, Thanksgiving, and December 25.

Books, Maps, and More Publications, maps, and other informative media may be purchased at information centers. These materials are sold by the Redwood Park Association and North Coast Redwood Interpretive Association, nonprofit organizations and close partners of these parks. Their work supports and enhances the information and education programs of Redwood National and State Parks. Portions of profits from their sales help support ranger-led programs, the free

Visitor Guide, and special projects. Donations by the Redwood Park Association and North Coast Redwood Interpretive Association made the production of this handbook possible.

Visitor Guide Pick up a copy of the free *Redwood National and State Parks Visitor Guide* at an information center. Published seasonally the *Visitor Guide* lists current ranger-led programs, scenic drives, special events, and more. Feature articles explore the parks' natural and cultural histories.

Accessibility Information about access for persons with disabilities also is available at information centers. All information centers are physically accessible to wheelchair users. Wheelchairs are not available, however.

Ranger-led Programs
Regularly scheduled, ranger-led programs are available during the summer season. Programs may vary throughout the season and also from year to year according to the budgets for these parks, which are set by Congress and the California legislature. Ask at information centers for what programs and activities will be offered during your stay. Weekly schedules also are posted in the state park campgrounds. Many programs occur at or start from information centers or campgrounds.

Ranger-led programs explore both the natural and cultural histories of these parks and their stunning variety of landscapes and seascapes—from mountain woodlands and open prairies, to ancient redwood forests, and ocean beaches and tidepools. Topics of campfire talks and guided walks may include redwood ecology, birds, bears, tidepools, forest life, indigenous Indian cultures, wildflowers, logging, restoring the landscape, and tides, currents, and other ocean phenomena.

Outdoor Schools
Redwood National and State Parks operate Wolf Creek Outdoor School in Humboldt County and Howland Hill Outdoor School in Del Norte County. Educational groups may rent the Wolf Creek School in summer—see phone numbers.

Redwood sorrel (bottom), *Salal* (top)

100

Lodging and Food Services Other than campgrounds Redwood Hostel offers the only lodging in the parks. Redwood Hostel is operated by the Golden Gate Council of American Youth Hostels in cooperation with Redwood National Park. Call the hostel—see phone numbers—for location, availability, and fees and reservations information. The hostel boasts spectacular ocean views and ready access to many miles of hiking trails.

Motels, lodges, cabins, resort lodging, and food services are available near the parks and in and around Trinidad and Orick in the south to Crescent City, Hiouchi *(high-oo'-chee)*, Gasquet *(gas'-key)*, and Patrick Creek in the north. Contact the Orick and Crescent City-Del Norte County chambers of commerce for more information—see phone numbers.

Campgrounds Campgrounds operated by the National Park Service, California State Parks, U.S. Forest Service, and Humboldt and Del Norte counties are shown on the maps in this handbook. Within Redwood National and State Parks all campgrounds with sites accessible by vehicle are operated by the state parks. The National Park Service and California Department of Parks and Recreation maintain a small number of primitive campgrounds that offer walk-in sites only—or are backpack camping sites that may require a backcountry permit. At primitive campgrounds you must park in a parking lot and walk at least a quarter to a half mile to a campsite. Little Bald Hills primitive campground doubles as a horseback camp (hitching rail and water available). All sites have fire rings and toilets. Use metal food caches where available, animal-proof food canisters, or hang your food properly—see Bear Country!

All campers should read and heed the information about precautions in Bear Country!

Camping Reservations You are strongly encouraged to make a campground reservation if you want to camp during the months of May through September in the state parks' campgrounds. Reservations may be made up to seven months before your arrival date by calling the campground reservation service—see phone numbers.

Public Campgrounds, South

In Prairie Creek Redwoods State Park
Elk Prairie Campground on Newton B. Drury Scenic Parkway off U.S. 101 accommodates tents or trailers up to 24 feet long and campers up to 27 feet long. Facilities include nature center, bookstore, showers, restrooms, picnic area, trails, hiker/bicyclist sites, trailer dump station, and evening campfire talks. No hookups. Accessible for persons with disabilities. Campground reservation code: PRAI.

Gold Bluffs Beach Campground on Davison Road (gravel) off U.S. 101 north of Orick. Vehicles towing trailers may not exceed 24 feet in combined length or eight feet wide. Motorhomes towing a vehicle must have a combined length of less than 24 feet. Facilities include solar showers, restrooms, trails, hiker/bicyclist sites. Strong winds are common here, but the bluff-backed, ocean-front setting is rare! No vehicles are allowed on the beach. No reservations; the campground operates on a first-come, first-served basis.

Public Campgrounds, North

In Del Norte Coast Redwoods State Park
Mill Creek Campground on U.S. 101 south of Crescent City. RV length may not exceed 31 feet; trailer length 27 feet. Facilities include showers, restrooms, hiker/bicyclist sites, trailer dump station, and trails. No hookups. Accessible for persons with disabilities. Campground reservation code: DELN.

In Jedediah Smith Redwoods State Park
Jedediah Smith Campground on U.S. 199 at Hiouchi. RV length may not exceed 36 feet; trailer length 27 feet. Facilities include showers, restrooms, river sites, picnic area, trails, hiker/bicyclist sites, and trailer dump station. No hookups. Accessible for persons with disabilities. Group site accommodates 50. Reservation campground code: JEDE.

Primitive Camping and Backpacking
Backpacking is popular on the Coastal and Redwood Creek trails. In six sections the Coastal Trail runs the length of these parks with stunning scenery, from redwood forests to open prairies, high bluffs overlooking the ocean, sandy beaches, and mixed forests. You may camp only in the designated campsites; first-come, first served.

The one exception is Butler Creek Primitive Camp in Prairie Creek Redwoods State Park. To camp there you must first get a permit from the Prairie Creek Visitor Center at Elk Prairie on Newton B. Drury Scenic Parkway.

Backpackers headed for the Redwood Creek Trail must first obtain a backcountry permit from the Redwood Information Center near Orick. Backpack camping is allowed on the gravel bars of Redwood Creek upstream from the first foot bridge all the way up to a quarter mile on either side of Tall Trees Grove. ***Please read and heed precautions under Bear and Cougar Country!*** (Ask about animal-proof food canisters at the Redwood Information Center.) Secure all valuables before leaving your vehicle at the trailhead. Lock them in the trunk or out of sight.

Year-round hiker/bicyclist campsites are located at Prairie Creek and Jedediah Smith Redwoods State Park campgrounds and in the summer at Mill Creek Campground in Del Norte Coast

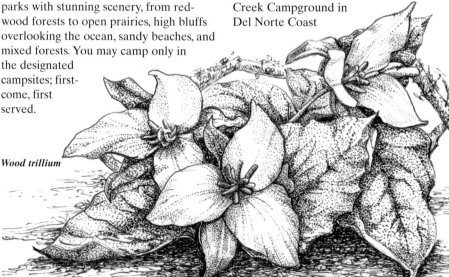

Wood trillium

Redwoods State Park. Reservations are not required; a modest fee is charged.

Many more trails suitable for backpacking await you on the national forest lands near these parks. Find information about them at the Smith River National Recreation Area Ranger Station in Gasquet or write to: Smith River National Recreation Area, Ranger Station, Gasquet, CA 95543.

Groceries and other camping items are available in Orick, Klamath, Crescent City, Hiouchi, and Gasquet.

Water Warning Purify all water from creeks, ponds, or lakes by heating it at a full boil for at least two minutes or by other approved methods such as filtering or using purification tablets.

Commercial Campgrounds Many commercial campgrounds provide a range of facilities within reach of Redwood National and State Parks. Most recreational vehicle and mobile home parks and tent-site campgrounds are clustered along U.S. 101 from Trinidad through Orick, Klamath, and Requa to north of Crescent City and along U.S. 199 at Hiouchi, Gasquet, and Patrick Creek. The facilities they offer vary. Some may include hookups, showers, laundry, cable TV, playgrounds, and propane. Others offer more traditional tent sites with table and grill or fireplace, and potable water and toilets available nearby. Some commercial campgrounds provide easy access to fishing, hiking trails, or other recreation and attractions. Chambers of commerce are the best sources of current information about these facilities—see phone numbers.

Riptides Swift currents, extremely cold water, and strong undertow (riptides) make swimming dangerous even on calm days. No lifeguards are stationed on the parks' 30 miles of beach. Check tide tables before walking on beaches to avoid becoming trapped. Watch children closely!

Tsunami Precautions A tsunami is a series of large sea waves usually caused by earthquakes beneath the ocean floor. Waves reaching up to 100 feet have surged inland along the shoreline here. If you feel a strong earthquake while on the coast, move to higher ground (at least 100 feet above shoreline) and move inland away from the coast right away and stay away. Don't return to the coast after the first wave—big waves can occur for hours—but wait for an offical "all clear" on the radio.

Beach Etiquette People and wildlife heavily use the parks' beaches. Respect others and help care for wild creatures by keeping dogs leashed. Collect only unoccupied seashells. Ocean fishing requires a valid California fishing license, and state regulations are enforced in the parks. Watch for vehicles on beaches. Report unsafe acts to a park ranger. Keep away from cliff edges. They can crumble and slide. Never throw rocks or other objects from bluffs; this endangers hikers below.

Marine Mammals and Injured Wildlife Never touch, molest, or otherwise interfere with marine mammals on beaches. Seals and sea lions often haul out on North Coast beaches. The young may rest on shore, while the parents swim nearby. Report any injured, dead, or beached seal, sea lion, or whale. Animal carcasses can carry infectious diseases. For your safety don't touch them.

Bear Country! If a bear learns it's easy to get food by hanging around humans that spells trouble. It spells *possible* trouble for humans. It spells potentially *fatal* trouble for the bear. It's a fact—proper food storage saves bears. Don't be bear careless! Do it right. Keep bears alive and wild.

Check at park information centers for information on campgrounds with bear-proof lockers. If your campground has no lockers, you may be able to borrow a bear-proof canister to pack in and protect your food. If bear-proof storage is not available, *know* how to hang food, garbage, and scented nonfood items *before* your trip.

Hang things 12 feet from the ground, 10 feet out from the trunk of the tree, and five feet below the branch. At some campsites bear poles are provided for hanging food and scented items. Pack out all garbage. Cook and store food at least 100 feet away from where you sleep. Wash dishes immediately after use.

Never feed bears (or any wildlife) or leave your food unattended. Use bear-proof garbage cans and food storage lockers. Put food and odorous items away right after eating. Store food and odorous items in your car trunk or hang them if camping away from your car. *Federal regulations require proper food storage in designated bear habitat.*

If a bear appears: *Stand up* and wave your arms. *Shout* and make other loud noises. Throwing small rocks in the bear's direction will usually send it running. Be bold but use good judgment. If the bear does anything that makes you feel threatened, *back* away. *Do not run.* And don't drop your pack.

If you see a bear please fill out a wildlife observation card at a park information center. Park biologists need your help to track bear sightings and current behavior.

Cougar Country! While the odds that you might see one of these extremely secretive animals are very low, cougars or mountain lions do roam throughout Redwood National and State Parks. They have been spotted in picnic areas and along trails and roads. Cougars once had probably the most extensive range of any land mammal in this hemisphere—from Canada through South America and from coast to coast. Since the 1920s they have been largely limited to the West because of hunting and habitat loss, but recently cougar sightings have been increasing in areas of the East, particularly where there are large populations of deer.

Cougars have been known to attack people and pets, but no attack has yet been reported in these parks. Nevertheless it is wise to be prepared. Read and heed the following:

Don't hike alone. Watch children closely and do not let them run ahead of you on the trail. Don't run. Mountain lions are likely to chase things that run, because they associate running with prey. If you encounter a mountain lion do not bend over or crouch down. Try to appear as big as possible. Hold your ground or slowly move away while facing the cougar. If you have little children with you pick them up without bending over. If the lion behaves aggressively wave your hands, shout, and throw sticks or stones at it. If attacked, face the cat and fight back.

Report any lion sightings to a ranger immediately. Call the general parks number or report it at an information center.

Just driving through? If so you're in luck —you can see a lot by auto touring here. And it's easy to combine auto touring with walking a short trail or a stretch of beach.

Paved Scenic Roads

Enderts Beach Road south of Crescent City off U.S. 101. Beach and trail access, tidepools, coastal views, whale watching, birding.

Requa Road just north of the Klamath River. Hiking trail, picnicking, whale watching. An outstanding view of the Klamath River entering the sea. Steep grades require cautious driving.

Newton B. Drury Scenic Parkway north of Orick off U.S. 101. Access to Prairie Creek Redwoods State Park and Elk Prairie, a favorite browsing area for Roosevelt elk. Tune your radio to 1610 AM in this area for elk information.

Big Tree Wayside off Newton B. Drury Scenic Parkway in Prairie Creek Redwoods State Park. Park at the wayside and walk the paved, 100-yard-long trail to a coast redwood tree measuring 304 feet tall and 21 feet in diameter.

Paved/Unpaved Scenic Road

Bald Hills Road north of Orick off U.S. 101. Access to Lady Bird Johnson Grove with one-mile trail through the redwoods. Elk viewing, oak woodlands, Tall Trees Grove access, prairies. Not recommended for motor homes or trailers because of its steep, 17-percent grade.

Coastal Drive south of Klamath River bridge. Eight-mile drive along river and ocean. Paved and unpaved sections alternate. Coastal views, hiking trails, whale watching, and picnicking. World War II historic site. Unpaved sections can be rough. Motor homes and trailers turn off at Alder Camp.

Unpaved Scenic Roads

Howland Hill Road near Crescent City, off U.S. 101—see map for road access from the west or east. A six-mile drive through Jedediah Smith Redwoods State Park gives access to a one-mile trail through Stout Grove. Watch for two-way traffic on this one-lane gravel road and beware of soft road shoulders. Motor homes and trailers are not advised.

Cal-Barrel Road north of Orick off Newton B. Drury Scenic Parkway. This three-mile drive through redwood trees has no turn-around for motor homes or trailers. It is open to mountain bikes.

Davison Road north of Orick off U.S. 101. A nine-mile drive through redwood and spruce forests to Gold Bluffs Beach and Fern Canyon. Walk a half mile into this intimately narrow, stream-carved canyon lined with ferns. This road also leads to trailheads for Prairie Creek Redwoods State Park. A day-use fee is collected. Vehicle length cannot exceed 24 feet.

Pacific rhododendron

Hiking Trails

Some 200 miles of walking and hiking trails await you in Redwood National and State Parks. What that fact alone cannot tell you is how many very different exploration adventures this offers. Ancient redwood and other forest types and open prairies meet mountains *and* sea coast here, so the natural diversity is remarkable. The best way to *feel* that diversity is on foot.

Hiking options appear in trail-guide pamphlets sold at information centers or by mail order from the Redwood Park Association and the North Coast Redwood Interpretive Association—see phone numbers. These give trail and trailhead locations, mileage, one-way trip time, features, and difficulty classification for more than 60 walks or hikes.

Bicycling and Horse Trails

Maps and information on trail conditions for bicyclists are available at information centers. Bicycles are allowed only on designated bicycle trails. Ask for details on the Holter Ridge Bike Trail, Rellim Ridge Trail, the Last Chance Section of the Coastal Trail, Little Bald Hills Trail, and the Prairie Creek-Ossagon Trail Loop. Have appropriate safety gear—trail surfaces are uneven, and tumbles do happen.

Redwood Creek Horse Trail is four loop trails and two designated stock campgrounds. Its trailhead is next to the Orick Rodeo Grounds. Any overnight stay at a stock-use campground requires a backcountry permit available from a Redwood National and State Parks visitor center.

Only pellets, cubes, or certified weed-free hay are allowed in campgrounds. No grazing is allowed. All park vegetation is protected. Stock animals must stay on designated stock trails only. Walk your stock when approaching any group of hikers or riders.

Trail Manners

Horses share some trails with bicyclists. Walk your bike past horses so you don't spook them. Hikers can share all designated bicyclist trails. Be courteous: call out to hikers as you approach. Please, no pets. They threaten, and can be threatened by, park wildlife. Pets, firearms, and motorized vehicles are prohibited on park trails.

Regulations No dogs, hunting, or firearms are allowed. No bicycles or motor vehicles are allowed on hiking or horse trails. Be careful with fire; fires are permitted in designated areas only.

Short Walks and Nature Trails

Stout Grove A ½-mile easy walk in a river-flat group of redwoods. The Stout Tree (345 feet tall) is the main feature of this walk. The paved trail from parking lot area to redwood flat is fairly steep. Stout Grove parking lot lies off Howland Hill Road, seven miles east of Crescent City. In summer access is also available from Jedediah Smith campground.

Simpson Reed Nature Trail A ¾-mile flat stroll on self-guiding nature trail with large redwood, octopus tree (hemlock), and many redwood-associated plants. Park on the shoulder of Highway 199 two miles west of Hiouchi Information Center (six miles east of Crescent City).

Lady Bird Johnson Grove and Nature Trail A one-mile easy walk on self-guiding trail through a beautiful ridgetop redwood grove. Distant view of the ocean. Picnic sites. Travel on Highway 101 to Bald Hills Road (½ mile north of Orick). Turn right and travel 2½ miles on Bald Hills Road.

Tall Trees Grove A strenuous 2⅔-mile round-trip walk to an alluvial redwood grove where the world's tallest tree was identified in 1963. The loop trail through the grove features towering redwoods, beautiful stands of bigleaf maple, and California laurel. Private vehicles need a free permit to reach the trailhead. Permits are issued on a first-come, first-served basis at the Redwood Information Center near Orick—see the map on pages 94-95 and phone numbers.

Sessile trillium (left),
Douglas iris (right)

Whale Watching

Most California gray whales travel more than 11,000 miles per year in the longest migration known for mammals. Migrating grays are the easiest whales to watch. They stay close to shore, usually safely out from the violent interface of land and sea. You may glimpse gray whales here in fall as they swim south to Mexico or return to Alaska in spring. The cows give birth to calves in shallow Baja California lagoons. Calves gain 200 pounds per day building fat for their first trip north. Good whale-watching spots include Redwood Information Center, Gold Bluffs Beach, and the Klamath River and Crescent Beach overlooks.

Being mammals, whales breathe air and nurse their young. They breathe through a blowhole atop their head. Watch for their spouting. When whales return to the surface to breathe they first spout, spraying a fine mist of condensed water vapor out their blowholes.

Deer fern

Armchair Explorations

The nonprofit Redwood Park Association and North Coast Redwood Interpretive Association sell books, maps, videotapes, art prints, notecards, and games about this region in the parks and by mail. Proceeds of sales benefit the national and state parks' visitor services and educational programs.

For a free list of sales items, ask at an information center or write to: Redwood Park Association, 1111 Second St., Crescent City, CA 95531; or North Coast Redwood Interpretive Association, Orick, CA 95555. Also see phone numbers. Here are select items:

Brown, Joseph E. *Monarchs of the Mist,* 1982.

Carranco, Lynwood, and John T. Labbe. *Logging the Redwoods,* 1979.

Eifert, Larry. *The Distinctive Qualities of Redwoods,* 1993.

Evarts, John, ed. *Coast Redwoods,* 1997.

Harris, Stanley. *Northwestern California Birds,* 1993.

Hewes, Jeremy. *Redwoods: The World's Largest Trees,* 1981.

Rasp, Richard. *Redwood, The Story Behind the Scenery,* 1990.

Rhode, Jerry and Gisela. *Redwood National & State Parks: Tales, Trails, & Auto Tours,* 1994.

Save-the-Redwoods League. *California Redwoods Parks and Preserves,* 1993.

— *Redwoods of the Past,* 1977.

— *Trees, Shrubs & Flowers of the Redwood Region,* 1984.

Schneider, Bill. *The Tree Giants,* 1988.

Webber, Bert and Margie. *Battery Point Light and the Tidal Wave of 1964,* 1991.

Credits

The National Park Service thanks all those persons who made the preparation and production of this handbook possible. Special thanks to the Redwood Park Association and North Coast Redwood Interpretive Association for financial support and to the staffs of Redwood National Park and the California State Parks. This handbook was prepared by the staff of the Division of Publications, National Park Service: Angie Faulkner, designer; Tom Patterson, cartographer; and Ed Zahniser, editor. Photos and artwork not credited below are from the files of Redwood National Park and the National Park Service. Some materials may not be reproduced without permission of their owners.

Ansel Adams 85
Dugan Aguilar 76
Frank Balthis 88
Virginia Brubaker drawings courtesy of Redwood Park Association 97-108
California State Library 79 mining
Calla Photography of objects courtesy of Del Norte County Historical Society 57 harpoon, 72, 74 baskets
Carr Clifton 10, 17
Del Norte County (Calif.) Historical Society 56-57 photos, 70, 75 basket maker
Marion J. Dalen 57 salmon
John Dawson 30-33, 42-43
John Elk III back cover
Jeff Gnass 54, 78-79
Carrie E. Grant 64-65 elk
John and Karen Hollingsworth 61 owl
Steve Homer 74-75 lodge
Tom and Pat Leeson 60 otter, 61 sea lions, mink, mountain lion, squirrel
Chuck Place 14-15, 22, 24-25, 41, 50
Redwood Park Association 67 top insert
Walt Saenger 52-53 both, 60 seal, 90-91
Save-the-Redwoods League 86 logo
Smithsonian Institution 59 harpoon from Handbook of North American Indians:

California, Anthropology Catalog #341274
Connie Toops 60 bloodstar
Larry Ulrich 2-5, 13, 26, 28-29, 46, 48, 55, 58, 60 slugs, 65 oaks, 68
George Wuerthner front cover, 8-9, 18

Library of Congress Cataloging-in-Publication Data

Redwood: a guide to Redwood National and State Parks, California / produced by the Division of Publications, National Park Service, U.S. Department of the Interior.
p. cm.—(Official National Park handbook, Redwood National and State Parks: handbook 154). Includes index.
1. Redwood National Park (Calif.)—Guidebooks. 2. Parks—California, Northern—Guidebooks. 3. Redwood—California, Northern. 4. Natural history—California, Northern—Guidebooks. I. United States. National Park Service. Division of Publications. II. Series: Handbook (United States. National Park Service. Division of Publications):
154.F868.R4R4   1997
917.94' 12—dc21
ISBN 0-912627-61-1

☆GPO 2010—357-935/80008 Reprint 2005

Index

National Park Service

The mission of the Department of the Interior is to protect and provide access to our nation's natural and cultural heritage and honor our trust responsibilities to tribes. The National Park Service preserves unimpaired the natural and cultural resources and values of the National Park System for the enjoyment, education, and inspiration of this and future generations. The National Park Service cooperates with partners to extend the benefits of natural and cultural resource conservation and outdoor recreation throughout this country and the world.